21st CENTURY LONG ISLAND

A History of the First 25 Years

RICHARD PANCHYK

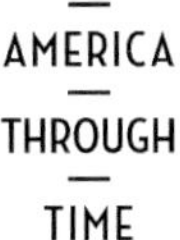

Thanks to Alan Sutton and Kena Smith at America Through Time
for their help and continued support.
Special thanks to Miranda for the brilliant idea for this book.

Photo credits: TK

America Through Time®
An imprint of Sutton Publishing Inc.
www.through-time.com

First published 2025

ISBN 978-1-63499-547-4

Typeset in Gotham Book
Printed and bound in England

Introduction

Time is constant, yet it does not always feel so steady. Our perception of how time passes changes not only based on what we are doing (aka the old saying, "time flies when you're having fun"), but also on what is going on in our world, and how we experience and process it all. Lately, our perception of time has become more skewed than ever, for a few important reasons.

These days, we Long Islanders collectively capture and share millions of moments every day. Where once we used film cameras to take photos mainly of the most important events, people, and places in batches of twenty-four or thirty-six at a double-price (the cost of the film and of the developing), now we have unlimited capabilities for capturing and viewing images at no cost. Our phones are filled with thousands of pictures of random moments throughout our days. Scrolling to find an image from even a month ago can be a Herculean effort. In preserving so many points in our daily lives, we have changed our perception of time and memory. Last week might seem much further away than it used to because through our image captures, we can constantly recall and relive moments otherwise quickly forgotten. Conversely, it might also feel closer in time for the very same reason.

How and when we access our images has also changed how we perceive time. In the past we would put our photos into a physical album that would find a place on our shelves at home. Now, we carry reminders of our lives with us at all times, accessible for reference at a moment's notice. We have practically stopped printing photos altogether. Even as the past is no longer permanent in the way it used to be, it is even more permanent and present than before; yet the sheer number of images we capture and share makes it seem more distant than before. We watch (and share) our kids growing up in increments of minutes not months, we document favorite meals, weird signs, and random moments for which we even forget the significance a few days later.

In addition, we experienced a major catastrophic event together that totally skewed our perception of time: the COVID-19 pandemic. The pandemic years altered time by changing our routines and lives drastically. From March 2020 to sometime in 2022, we lived in anywhere from full to partial limbo, as fear and hope mingled together on a daily basis as we tried to make it through. I documented this strange time in my book *Garden City: Pictures from a Pandemic* (2021). How many times since have we used COVID as a time marker? "When was that concert?" we might say to a friend. "It must have been pre-COVID, maybe 2018 or 2019?" And then we marvel at how it could have been that long ago and how we can remember events from the summer of 2016 more clearly than from the summer of 2020.

With the altered sense of time, we have also lost some of our ability to fully process events in a normal way, instead digesting them through social media and soundbites. Where in the past, news was limited to the space within the finite pages of a newspaper or the half-hour of a news program on television, cable television and then the internet changed all that. There are no longer limits to how much coverage a topic gets—or how many and what types of topics get coverage. Our search engines and phones even customize the news we see based on our preferences. In being so specialized, news becomes a strangely personalized experience. Objectively major stories are juxtaposed with minor ones from sources ranging from unimpeachable to highly questionable. With all this "news" coming at us from various directions, we will actually miss some stories entirely because they did not appear high enough in our social media feeds or we were "off the grid" for even a matter of hours.

The other factor that has happened recently is a globalizing of our news. No longer are we exposed to all the events of our towns and villages as we used to when subscribing to our local papers; we process events on a larger scale than we used to, and the local component of our news is minimized to an extent, and what we see these days often depends on what topics we have recently searched.

This book tries to rewind and look back at some of the important events of the first twenty-five years of the twenty-first century on Long Island. In pulling these together, I have tried to be at least a little bit more objective than your social media feed or Google news, and I have curated this collection of moments as representative of different types of important events and moments impacting Long Island between 2000 and 2025. This is by no means comprehensive, but rather a (hopefully) good sampling of what happened, what affected us, what we experienced and lived through. And though the book covers the recent history of Long Island, due to the factors listed above, much of what is within these pages may feel like it happened forever ago. History is 2022, not just 1922. This new take on "local history" recognizes that the speed of modern life has skewed how we experience time. So fasten your seatbelts and let's take a journey through the opening years of this century. Note that a few of these events are ongoing and their stories will continue to change after the book is published; this volume documents their status as of the beginning of 2025.

21st Century Long Island

Baseball Comes to the Island (2000)

Playing at what was initially called EAB Park (and as of 2025 known as Fairfield Properties Ballpark) in Central Islip, the Long Island Ducks were Long Island's first professional baseball team. Co-founded by former Mets shortstop, 1973 championship hero, and manager Bud Harrelson (1944–2024) in 2000, the team has been host to many famous ex-(and future) major league ballplayers over the years—including most recently its manager Wally Backman, who was the second baseman for the World Series champion 1986 Mets and had a lifetime .275 average over fourteen years in the majors. A recent member of the Ducks was former Mets second baseman (2008–2015) and lifetime .296 hitter Daniel Murphy, who was trying to mount a comeback in 2023. Murphy batted .331 in thirty-seven games for the Ducks, then retired from baseball after playing for the Angels AAA affiliate later in 2023. As of 2025, the manager for the Ducks was Lew Ford, who holds the record for most seasons with the Ducks (thirteen) and most hits (1,002). Since the team was founded, more than 9 million fans have attended Ducks games at the 6,000-seat stadium, an Atlantic League record. The Ducks, like many minor league teams, are known for their family atmosphere and fun promotions, including fireworks and heritage nights, as well as promotional giveaways of baseballs, posters, tee shirts, caps, and baseball cards.

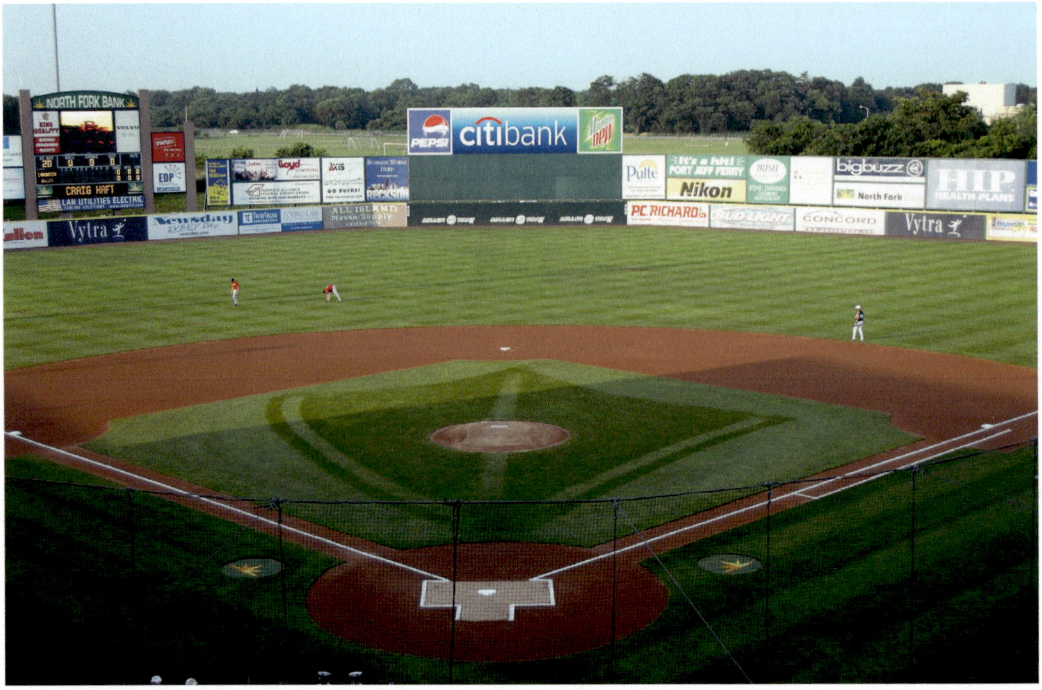

The Long Island Ducks ballpark in 2006. It was then known as Citibank Park; as of 2025, it is called Fairfield Properties Ballpark. It can hold about 6,000 spectators.

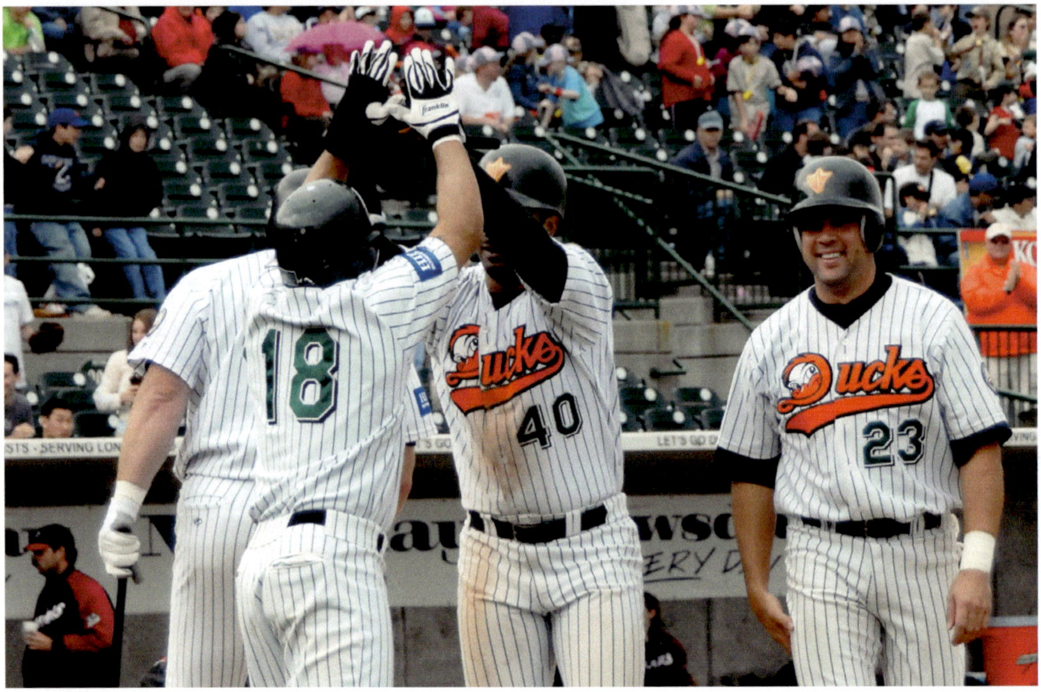

An image from a Ducks game on May 21, 2006.

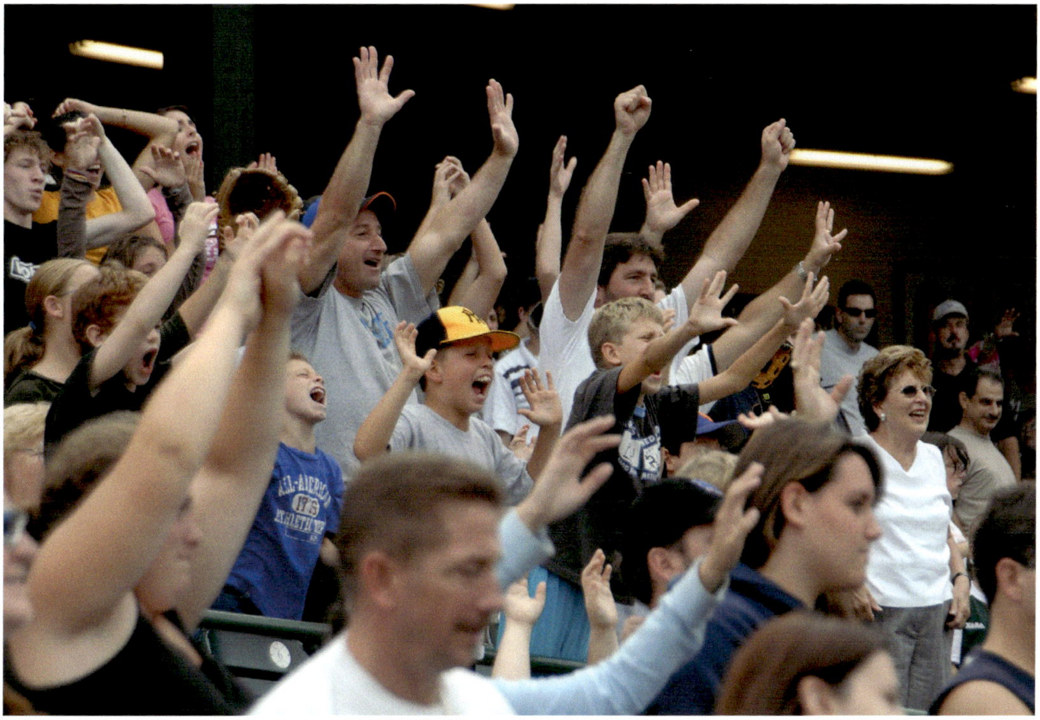

Ducks fans cheering on their team.

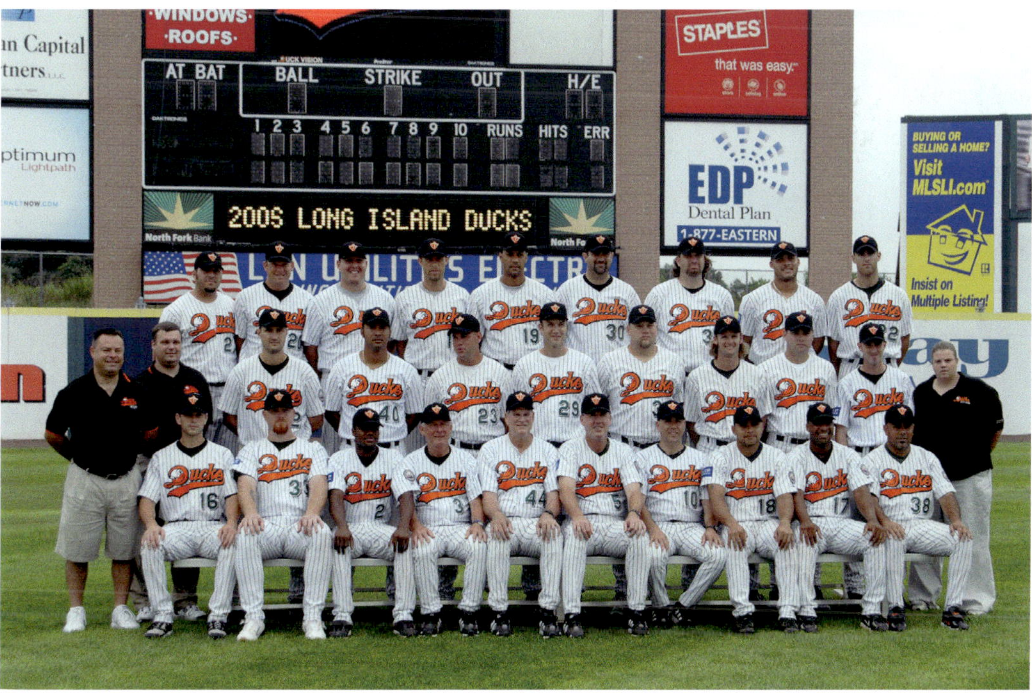

The 2006 Long Island Ducks team included former Major Leaguers such as Pat Mahomes (father of Kansas City Chiefs star quarterback Pat Mahomes), Henry Rodríguez, Tony Fiore, Mike Crudale, Bill Pulsipher, Erick Almonte, and Pat Ahearne (who led the team in pitching with twelve wins).

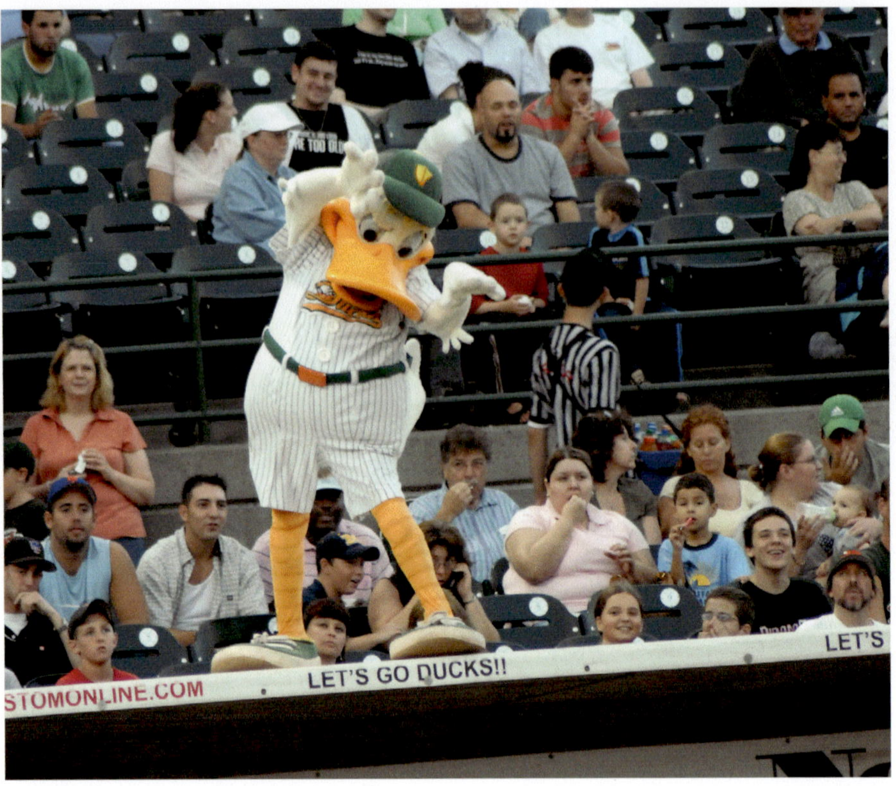

The Ducks mascot is, appropriately, a duck.

The Long Island Aquarium (2000)

Located on 3.2 acres along the Peconic River, the Long Island Aquarium is one of the most popular attractions on the east end. Construction began in the spring of 1999 and the aquarium opened on June 15, 2000, as Atlantis Marine World (the name changed to Long Island Aquarium in 2011) along the waterfront. It was the first major new aquarium to open in New York state since the 1960s, and it was also one of the first completed pieces in the revitalization of Riverhead's downtown area. The aquarium displays use more than 1 million gallons of water. Exhibits are both outdoors and indoors, and include penguins, sea lions, seals (at the entrance to the aquarium), stingrays, sharks, octopi, and electric eels. One of the most popular displays is the 12-foot-high shark tank. The aquarium also features one of the Western Hemisphere's largest all-living coral reef displays. Visitors are treated to daily events such as the sea lion shows. There are also non-marine animals on display, such as snakes, marmosets, owls, monitors, coatis, and porcupines. Another popular non-marine attraction is the indoor tropical butterfly garden.

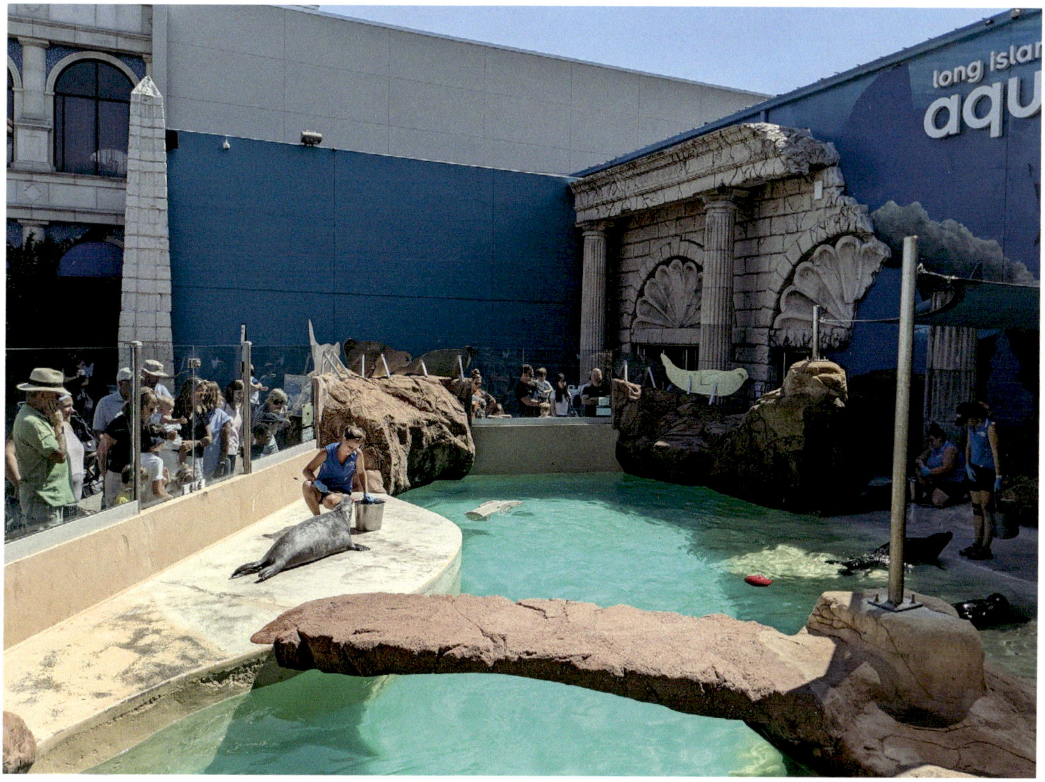

Feeding the sea lions at the Long Island Aquarium in 2022.

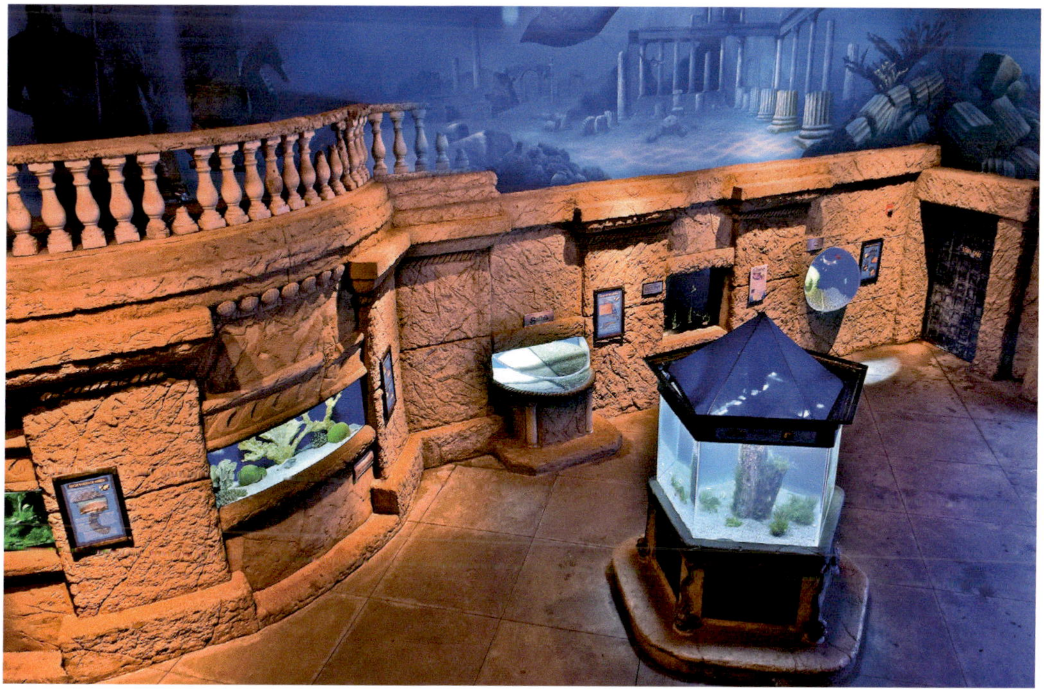

Exhibits in the aquarium in 2015.

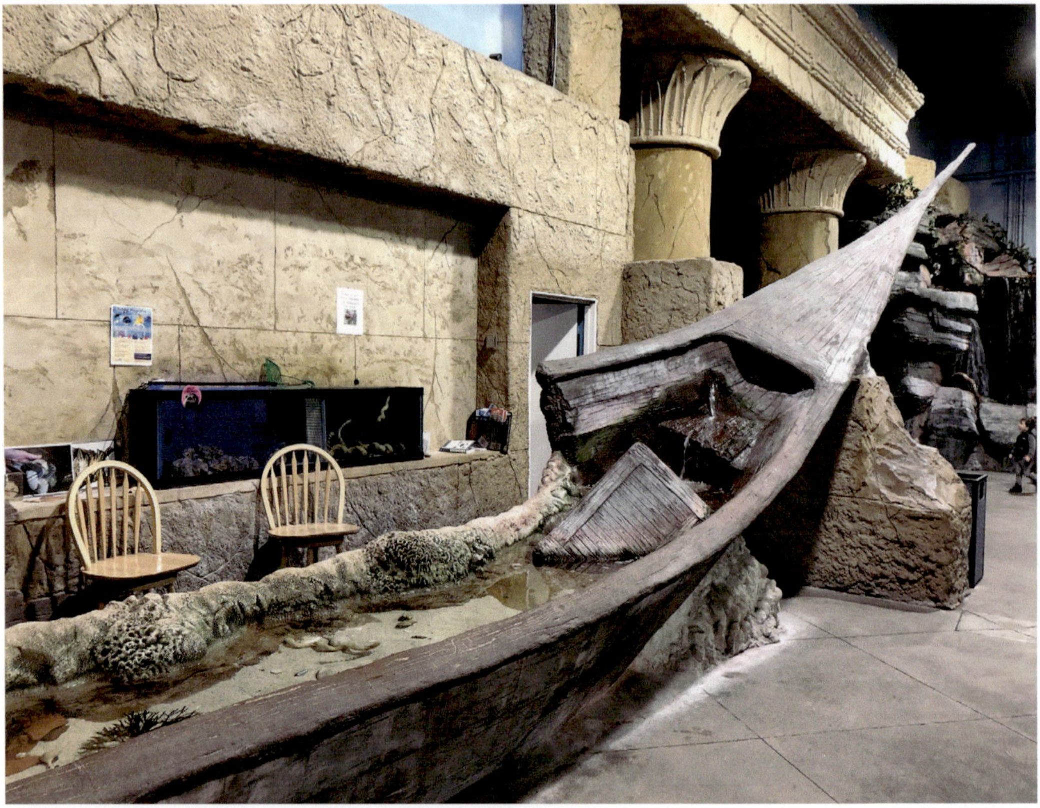

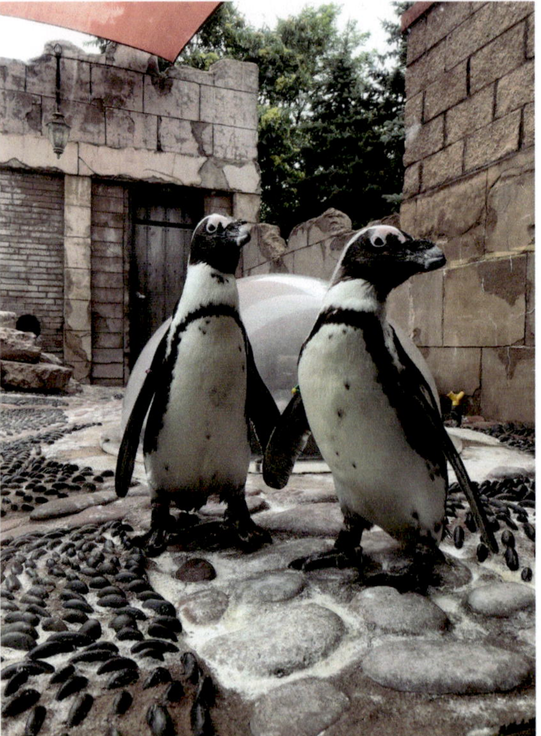

Above: The Touch Tank in the aquarium, 2019.

Left: Penguins, seen here in 2018, are just one of the many species living at the aquarium complex.

American Airpower Museum (2000)

During World War II, the Bethpage/Farmingdale area was one of the country's most important manufacturing hubs for fighter planes. Companies such as Fairchild Republic and Grumman turned out thousands of warplanes that were sent to the front lines to help the Allies make advances in both the European Theater and the Pacific Theater from massive factories. Though the industry died out by the end of the twentieth century, and much of the acreage that had been devoted to the aircraft industry was repurposed for commercial and office space, a new museum to celebrate the area's wartime heritage opened in 2000, just off New Highway in Farmingdale. Located adjacent to the still-thriving Republic Airport, the American Airpower Museum features a collection of vintage World War II planes, some of which still fly (and offer visitors the opportunity to experience flying in a vintage plane for a fee). When the museum first opened there were 5.7 million living World War II veterans in the United States; by the end of 2024, that number was estimated to be only 70,000.

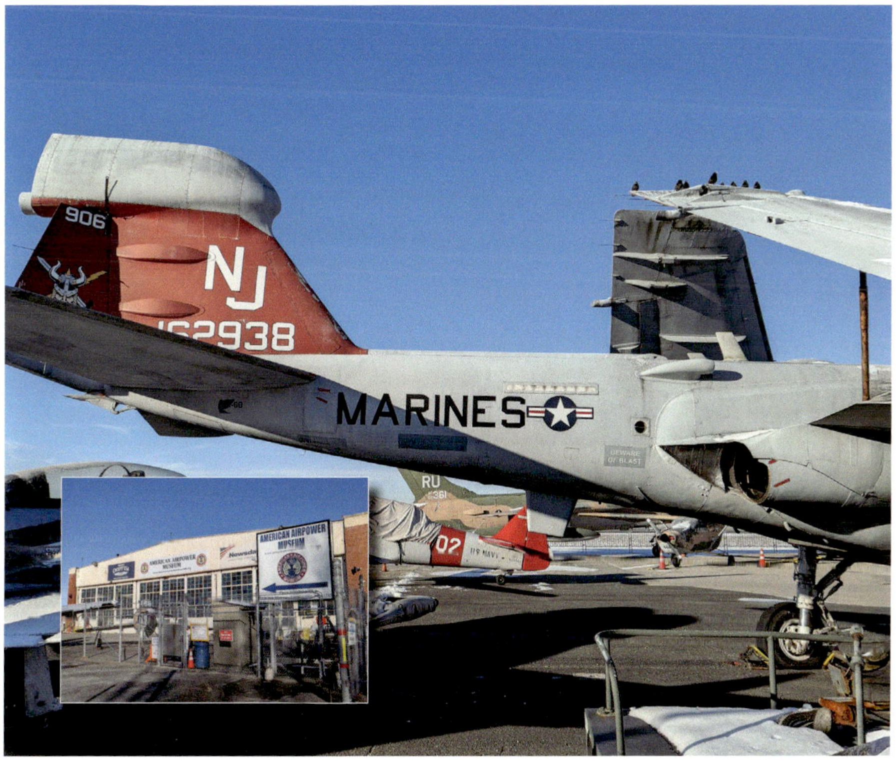

A vintage warplane on display at the American Airpower Museum in Farmingdale (see inset).

9/11 (2001)

Long Islanders answered the call when the horror of 9/11 happened that Tuesday morning in 2001—Nassau County sent 8,509 firefighters to the scene from its seventy-one volunteer fire departments and Suffolk County sent 1,000 firefighters from its 109 fire departments, many of whom arrived to the site quickly. Long Island police were also a presence at Ground Zero. As the tragic events unfolded, a total of 497 Long Islanders died at the site of the Twin Towers that day. In addition, there have been many deaths of first responders (and site cleanup personnel who worked in the rubble in the days and weeks that followed) due to 9/11-related illnesses, such as cancer from inhaling and being in close proximity to toxic dust and debris. Today, memorials to 9/11 are in several places on Long Island, notably at the lake in Eisenhower Park where a wall of remembrance lists the victims from Nassau County, and two aluminum tower sculptures rise. On March 11, 2003, President Bush, then-Gov. George Pataki, and former New York City Mayor Rudy Giuliani took part in the groundbreaking ceremony for the memorial. The memorial was dedicated on September 9, 2007. Steel beams recovered from Ground Zero were shipped to many locations around the country to serve as reminders and memorials to the lives lost made that day. There are more than eighty sites across Long Island that have a steel beam memorial, many of them firehouses, but also at a variety of other sites ranging from the Rocky Point VFW to the Knights of Columbus in Levittown to the Bay Shore Union Free School District.

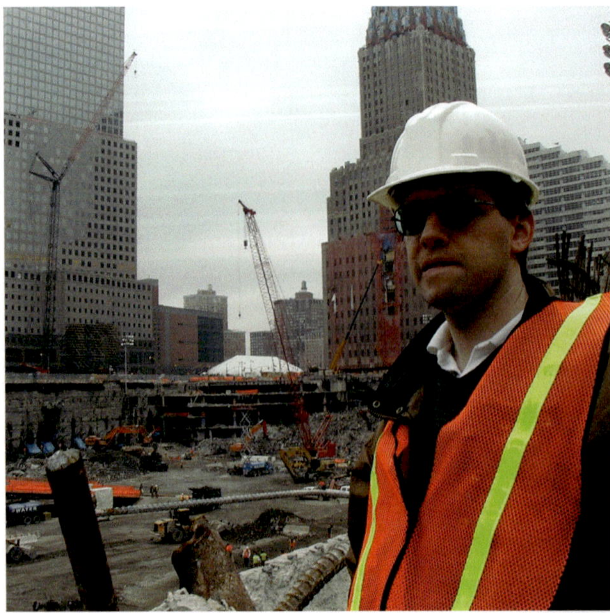

The author at Ground Zero in April 2002.

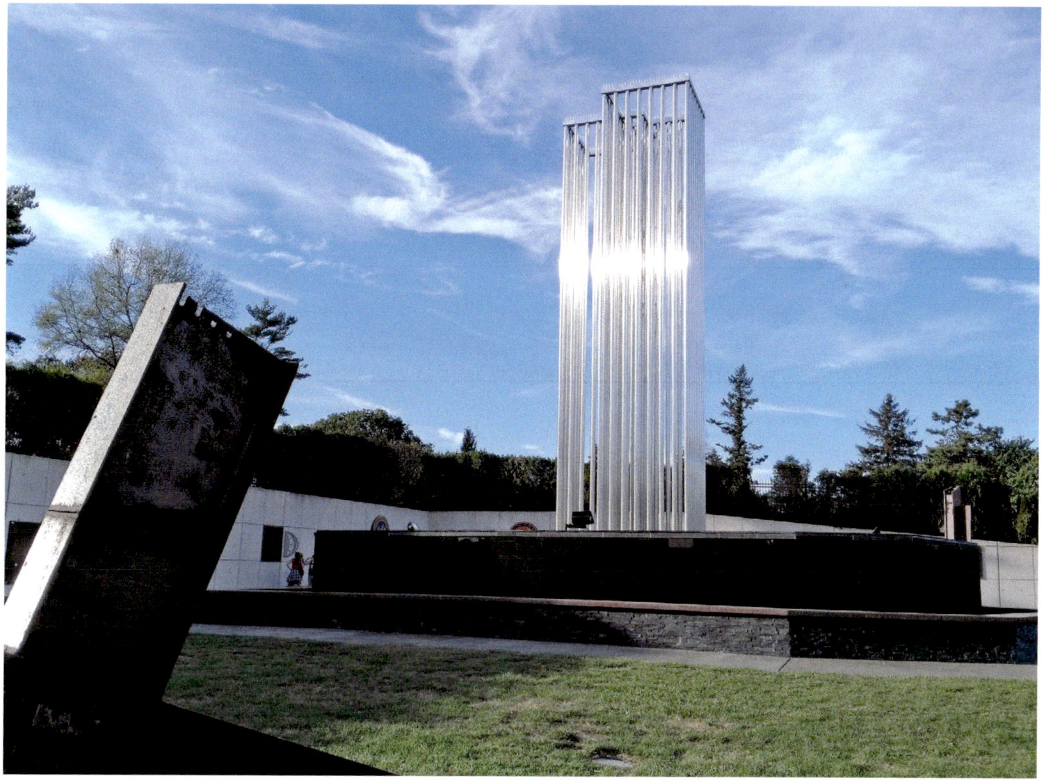

The 9/11 Memorial at Eisenhower Park, seen here on September 11, 2016.

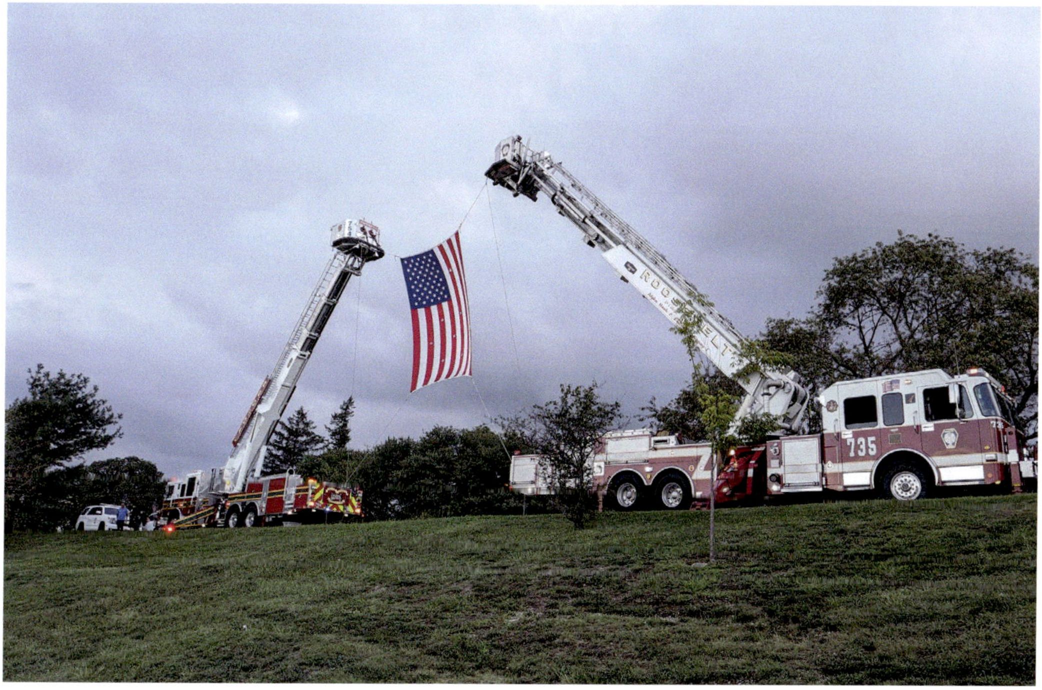

Fire engines hang a flag during the Eisenhower Park remembrance ceremony on September 11, 2023.

The Cradle of Aviation Museum (2002)

Though the first flight took place at Kitty Hawk, North Carolina, in 1903, aviation on Long Island began in earnest in 1909 with Glenn Curtiss flying from a makeshift field at Mineola. The surrounding area soon served as the "cradle of aviation" with many pioneering and record-breaking flights happening on the Hempstead Plains in the twenty years that followed, including the first licensed female pilot in the country in 1911, the first air mail flight also in 1911, and the start of Charles Lindbergh's famous transatlantic solo flight in 1927. What started as several flying fields in the area evolved into two main ones: the civilian Roosevelt Field and its neighbor to the south, the military air base called Mitchel Field (where Babe Ruth once caught a baseball dropped from an airplane). The former closed in 1950 and the latter in 1961 due to the encroachment of residential neighborhoods and the opening of much larger airports elsewhere. Despite this incredible heritage, only a few scant remnants of the area's heritage in flight still existed by the turn of the twenty-first century. Thankfully, a museum was built in a restored Mitchel Field hangar, celebrating aviation history on Long Island. It contains more than seventy-five aircraft and spacecraft that tell the story of local aviation. The museum has become one of Long Island's top attractions. The Firefighters Museum and the Children's Museum also opened there in former hangars, creating Long Island's first "museum row." Besides its function as a museum, the venue has also hosted various special events over the years. In 2023, Florida governor Ron DeSantis gave a speech there at the start of his ill-fated run for president.

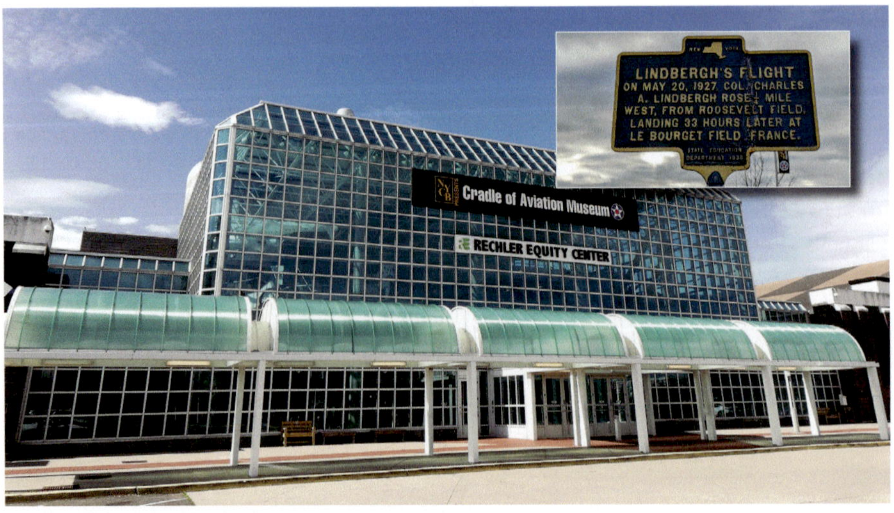

The Cradle of Aviation Museum opened in 2002 in Garden City in renovated hangars that used to be part of the Mitchel Field Air Base complex. Inset: The sign that used to be on the site where Lindbergh's plane took off was relocated to the Cradle of Aviation parking lot.

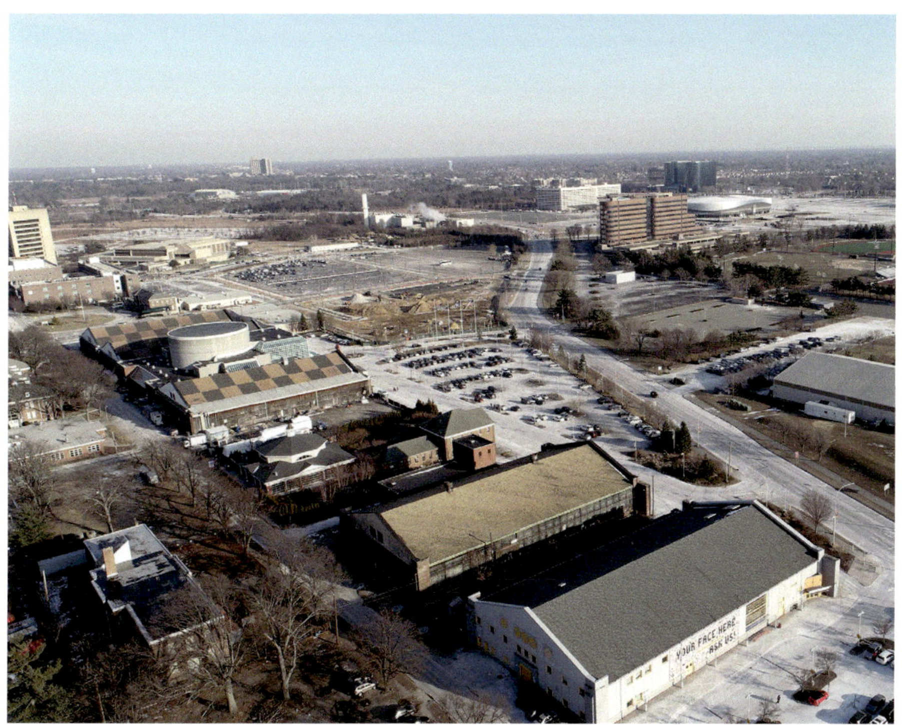

An aerial view of the Cradle of Aviation Museum (checkered hangars). Next to the museum to the right is Nunley's Carousel, a storage hangar, and a hangar converted into the Long Island Children's Museum.

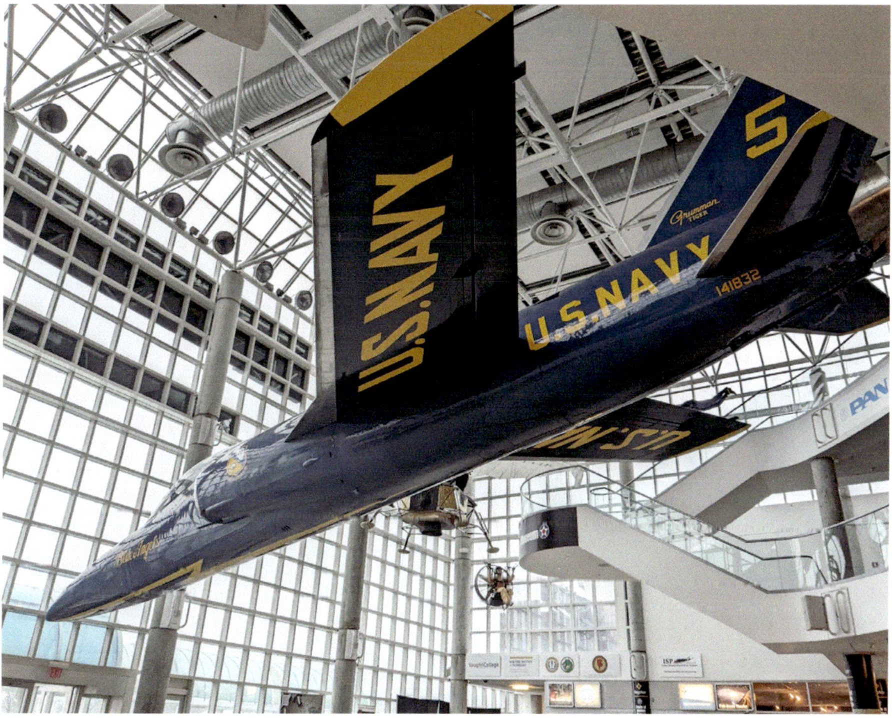

Planes hang from the ceiling of the Cradle of Aviation Museum lobby.

Long Island Music Hall of Fame (2004)

Dozens of popular musicians and music industry giants were either born in or lived on Long Island, including such greats as George M. Cohan, who lived in Great Neck, and Hicksville native Billy Joel, who named an album after Cold Spring Harbor. WBAU, the now-defunct Adelphi University radio station, is where rappers Public Enemy and Flava Flav got their starts. Long Island finally got its own Music Hall of Fame in 2004 and began honoring the locals who have made a difference in the music industry. Some of the musicians who have been inducted since the Hall of Fame opened include Lou Reed, the Ramones, Simon and Garfunkel, Blue Oyster Cult, Pat Benatar, Harry Chapin, Taylor Dayne, Debbie Gibson, Steve Vai, Billy Joel (and members of his band), and Joan Jett. Other inductees have included record company executives, promoters, and radio personalities. The inductions had been held at various locations (including The Space at Westbury) until 2022, when the LIMHOF got its own building in Stony Brook. In November 2023, a new exhibit opened there, called "Billy Joel—My Life, A Piano Man's Journey—The Ultimate Exhibition," which according to the LIMHOF website offers "over 50 years of Billy Joel's most cherished items." The limited exhibition was extended to run through the spring of 2025.

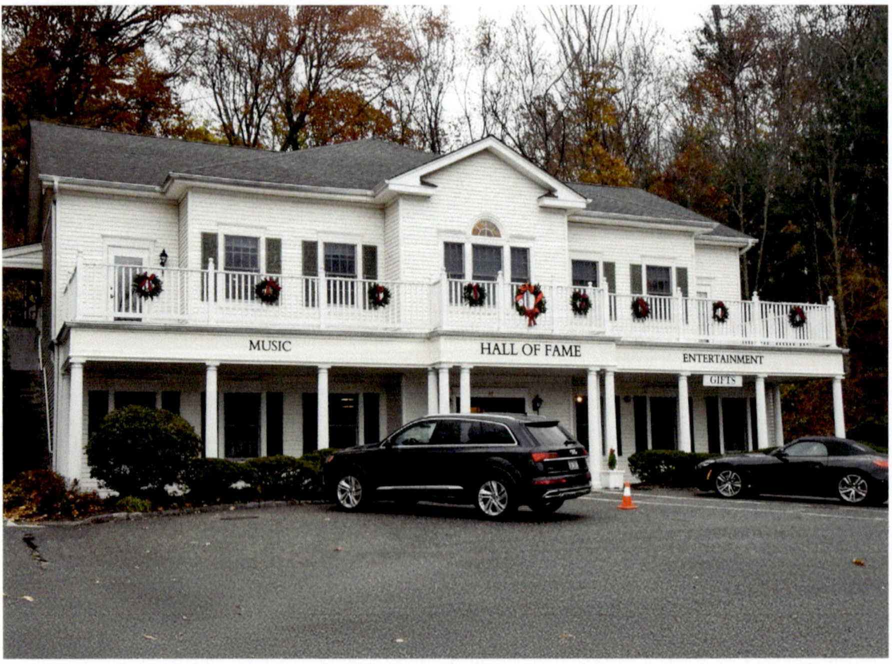

The Long Island Music Hall of Fame (LIMHOF), founded in 2004, found a brick-and-mortar home in Stony Brook in 2021.

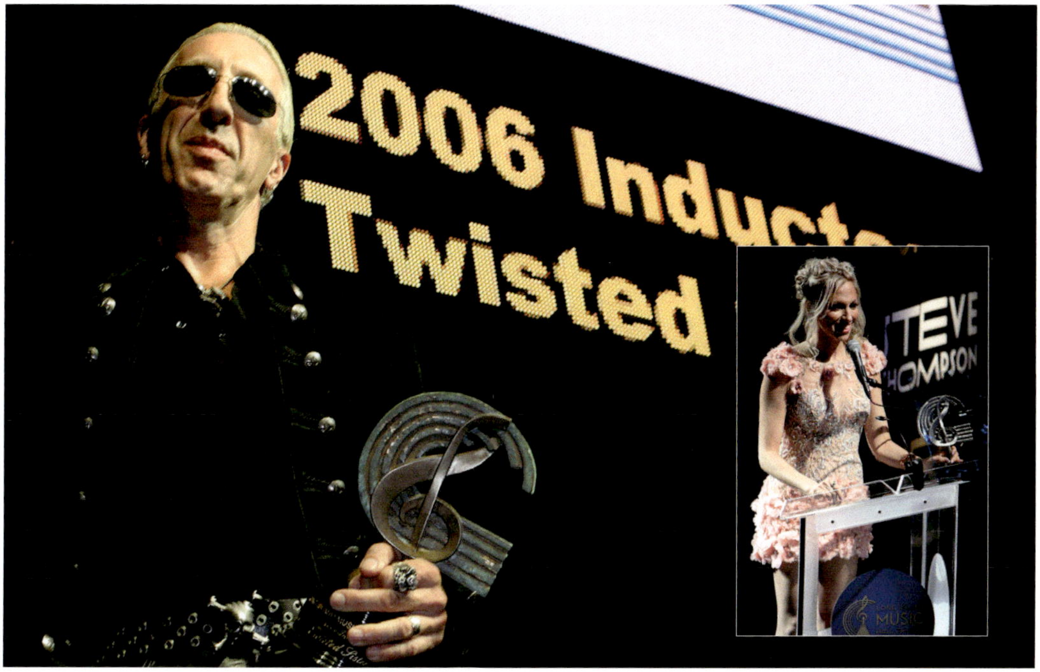

Dee Snider of Twisted Sister at his 2006 induction into the Long Island Music Hall of Fame. Inset: Singer Debbie Gibson at her induction ceremony in 2014.

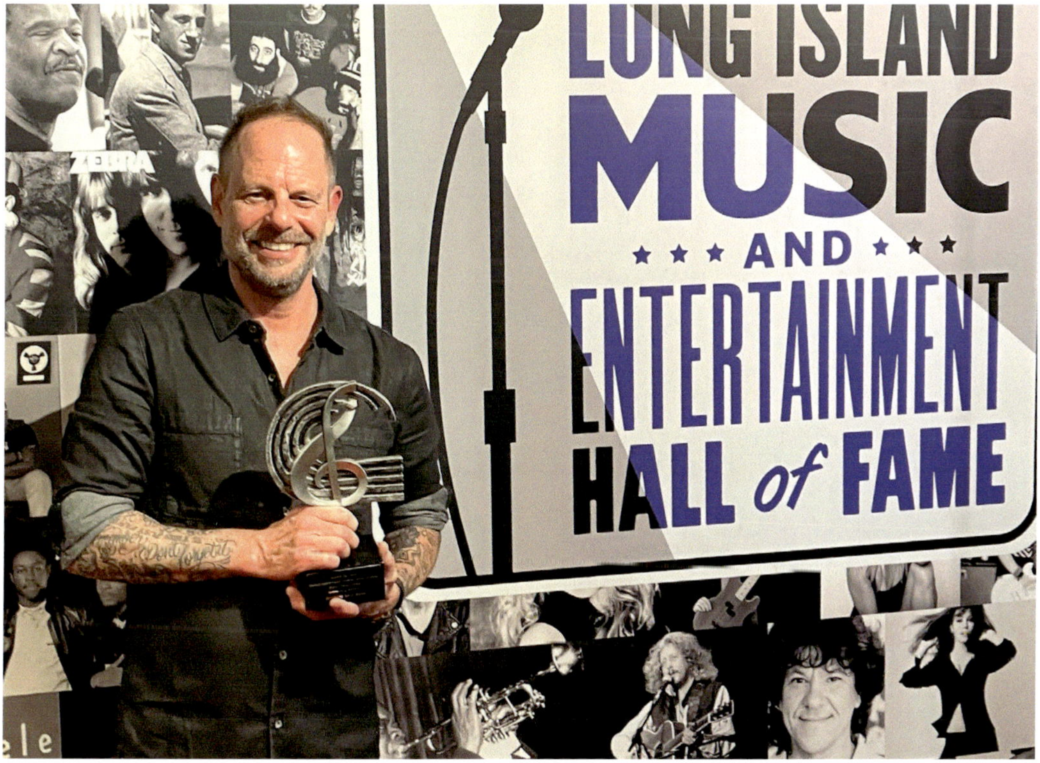

Vocalist Robin Wilson of the Gin Blossoms at his induction ceremony in 2023.

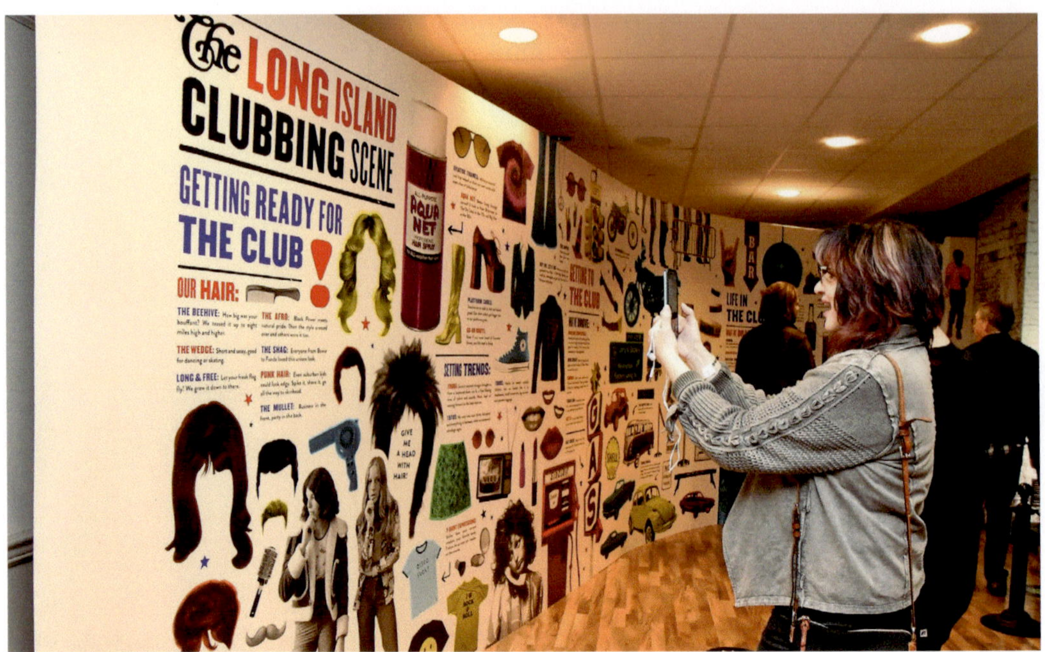

An exhibition on the Long Island clubbing scene in the newly opened LIMHOF building in 2022.

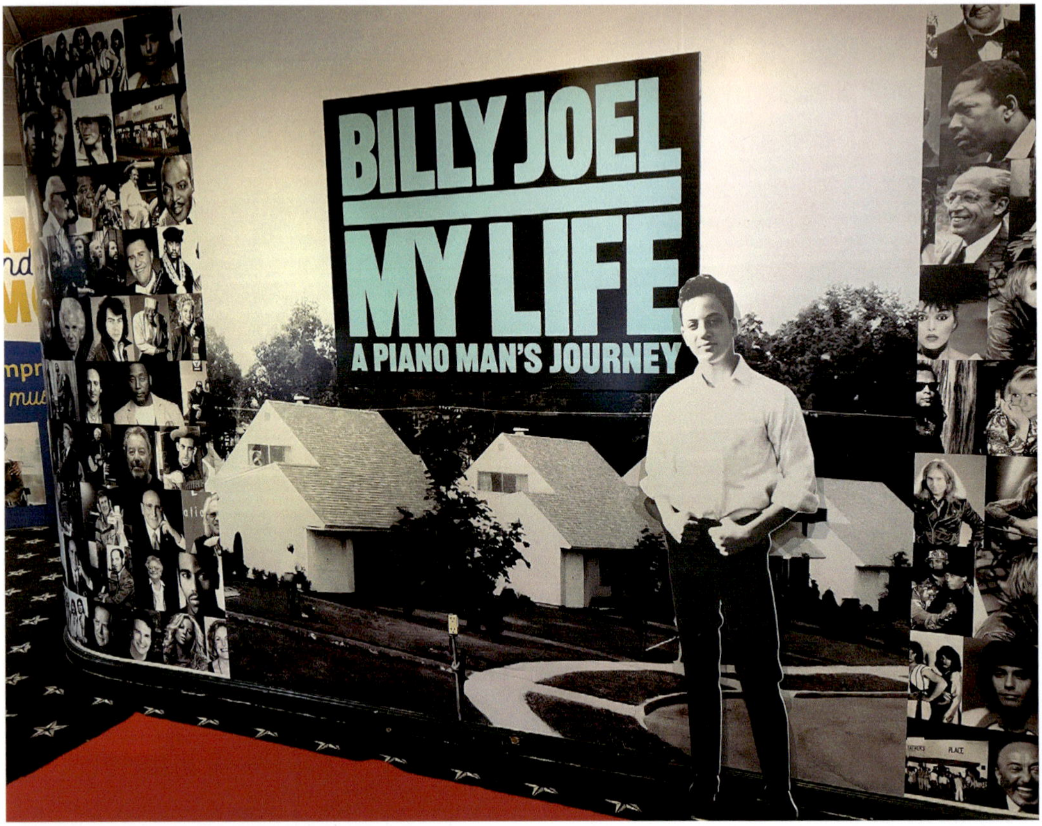

The title wall of the special Billy Joel exhibit at LIMHOF, running through 2025.

Farewell Jones Beach Restaurant (2004)

The original Jones Beach restaurant on the boardwalk opened in 1935 on the Central Mall near the water tower and Parking Field 4, and it was very popular with beachgoers. In 1963, the restaurant served up nearly 90,000 meals during the summer. The original building burned down in 1964 despite the efforts of eighty firemen who were on the scene within ten minutes, and it was replaced with a new and much larger restaurant in 1968. That building was in turn demolished in 2004 after decades of wear and tear from exposure to the marine environment. In 2006, plans were announced for a new 38,560-square-foot restaurant (capacity 400 diners) called Trump on the Ocean, but the project was stalled for years in a dispute with the state over variances for a basement. An agreement on the proposed 400-seat restaurant was finally reached in 2012, but later that same year the site was damaged by Hurricane Sandy and the project was abandoned. Today, a $30 million structure completed in 2019 and housing a Boardwalk Café (much smaller than the original restaurants) sits on the exact spot where the old restaurant used to be. The building sits on pile foundations due to the sandy soil in the area and elevation requirements to have it 20 feet above sea level.

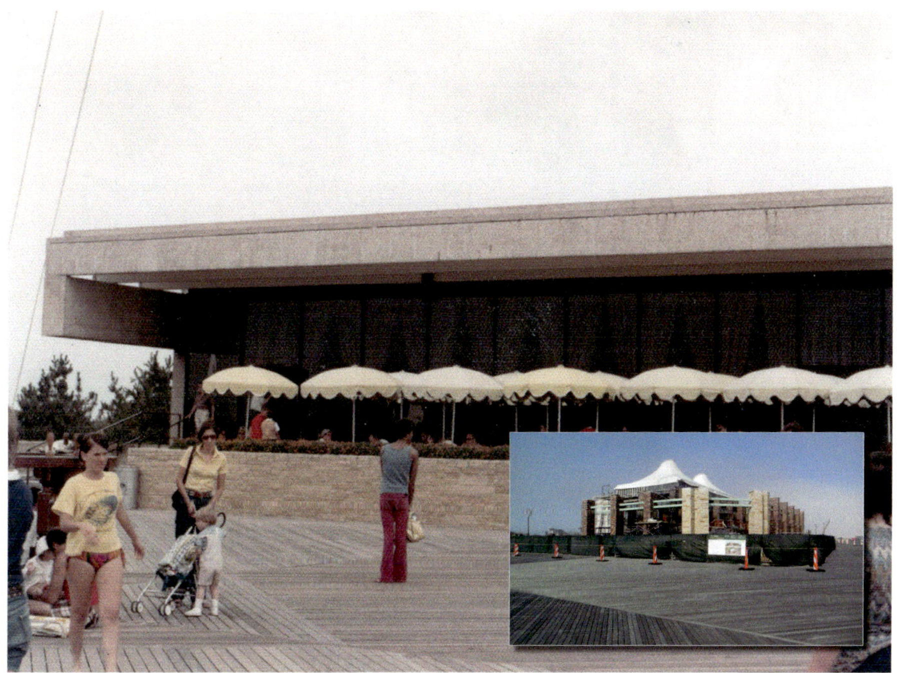

The old Jones Beach Restaurant, dating to the 1960s, was demolished in 2004 and the site stood vacant for years until a new structure was put in its place.

Gold Coast Ghosts (2006)

Long Island's mansion-filled Gold Coast along the north shore of Nassau and Suffolk counties reached its peak during the 1920s, pre-Stock Market crash. With World War II and the subsequent suburbanization and development of much of the island, many of the great estates were sold or subdivided. The burden of upkeep became too great. The first quarter of the twenty-first century saw the true end of an era. One of the last children who grew up in classic-era Gold Coast mansions was Peggy Phipps (1906–2006), founder of Old Westbury Gardens and daughter of Jay Phipps (1874–1958), who lived in the famous mansion that was featured in the Hitchcock movie *North by Northwest* (1959). She continued to live in a cottage on the property until her death. Her passing was symbolic of the ending of an era on Long Island. Some mansions had been demolished while others were repurposed; the Pratt mansion in Glen Cove became the Holocaust Memorial & Tolerance Center, for example. One of the last of the great estates still owned by the original family was Old Westbury's Erchless, a late Gold Coast addition that was built in 1935 (and one of the last Gold Coast estates to be built) by Howard Phipps (1881–1981), the younger brother of Jay Phipps and still owned by Howard's son, Howard Phipps, Jr. (born 1934); but an end was in sight to that legacy. The 92-acre estate was listed for sale in March 2024, at a price of $23 million (after a failed sale a few years earlier) and sold in December 2024 for $21 million. Taxes for the fifteen-bedroom, twelve-bathroom house and grounds were listed at $757,769 per year; included in the prospectus was a map showing how the property could be subdivided into thirty-two single-family minimum 2-acre lots as allowable by local zoning laws.

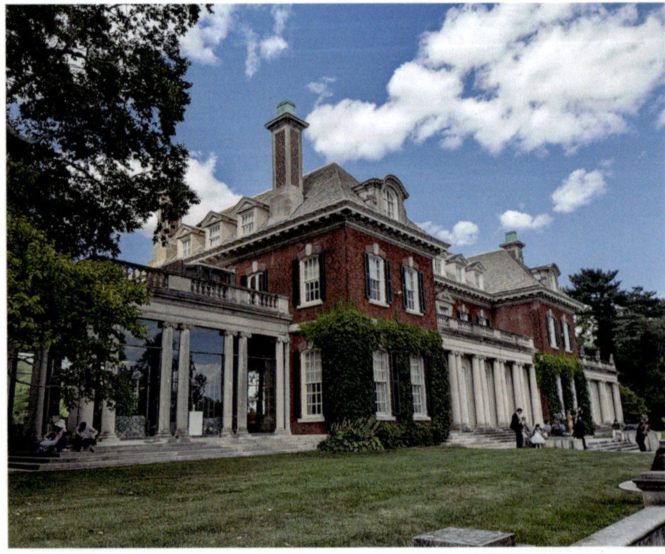

Westbury House, the mansion at Old Westbury Gardens. The last surviving child of the Phipps family died in 2006 at the age of 100.

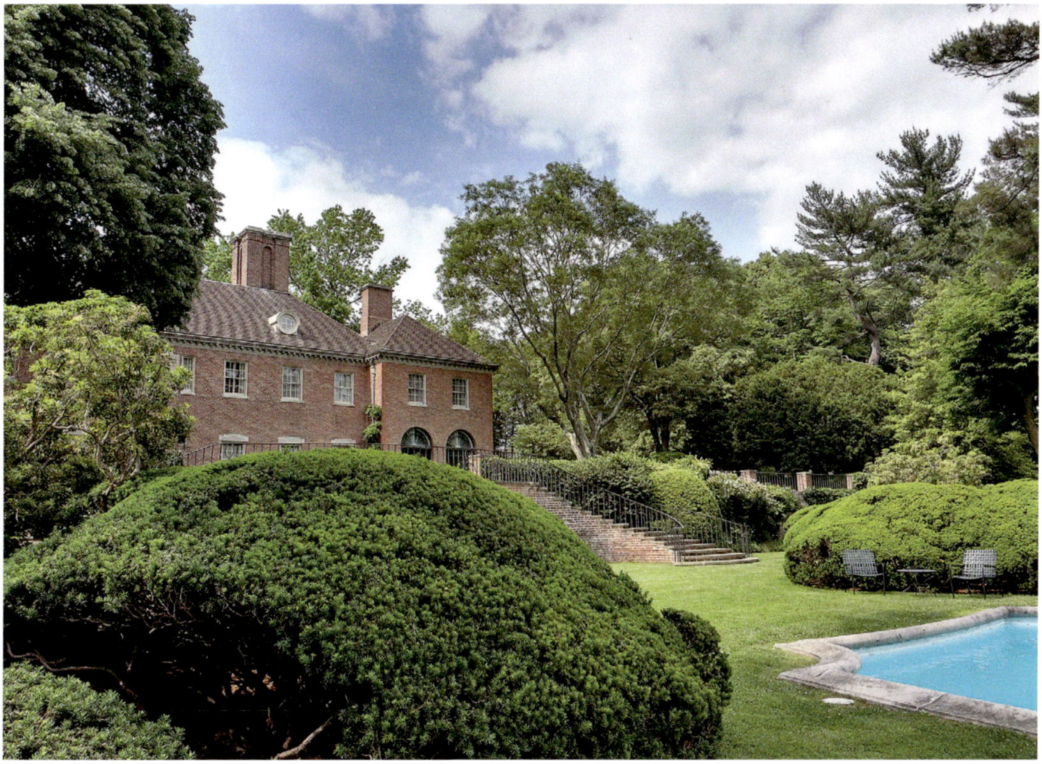

Erchless, the Howard Phipps estate, remained in the original family from 1935 until it sold in 2024.

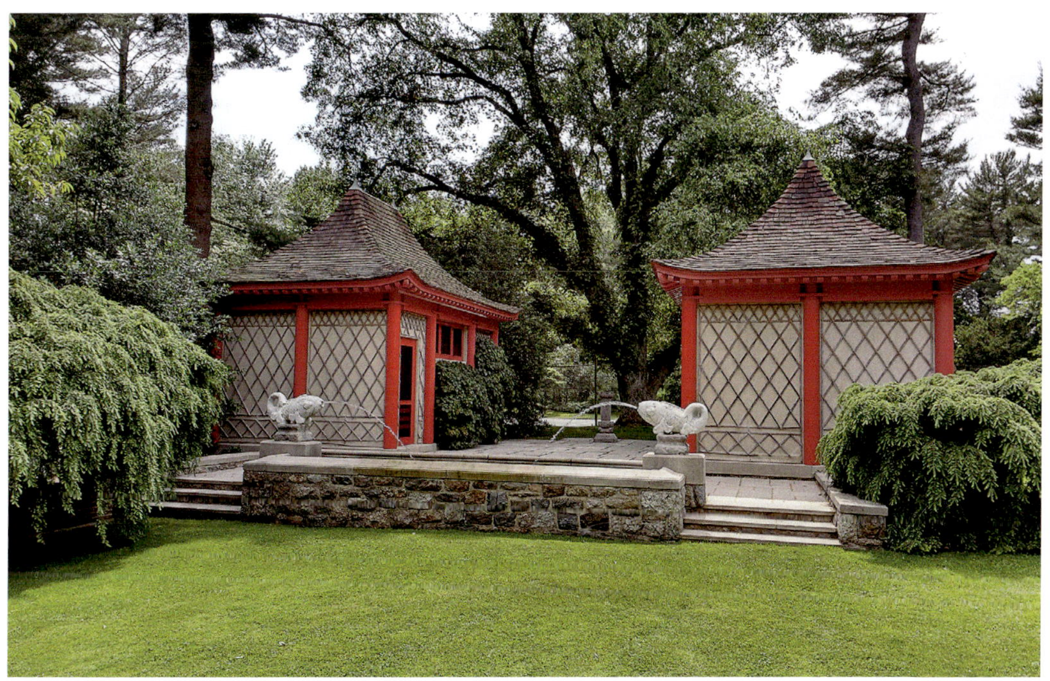

The Japanese pagoda-style changing rooms adjacent to the swimming pool at Erchless are an example of the extravagance that was the Gold Coast.

Last Grumman Tomcat Flies (2006)

Grumman Industries (now Northrup-Grumman) was founded in 1930 and moved to Bethpage in 1936. The company bought land bordering South Oyster Bay Road on the west, from the LIRR tracks south to the intersection with Route 107. At the time, Bethpage was a semi-rural community of farms. It was the perfect place for a large operation to manufacture fighter planes for the United States government. As the country ramped up its defense with the start of World War II, the Grumman complex grew to include several factory buildings, testing facilities, hangars, and runways and taxiways. During the war, there were about 25,000 employees at the Bethpage complex. Grumman's most famous World War II aircraft was the navy carrier-based F6F Hellcat. Over 12,000 of these powerful planes were produced in just two years. Grumman continued to be strong through the Cold War, and it was heavily involved in the space program since 1962, building thirteen lunar modules (one of which is on display at the Cradle of Aviation Museum a few miles to the west), but things slowed and staff cuts reduced the workforce to 3,000 by 1996. After Grumman sold off land, the property was repurposed. Shiny new buildings,

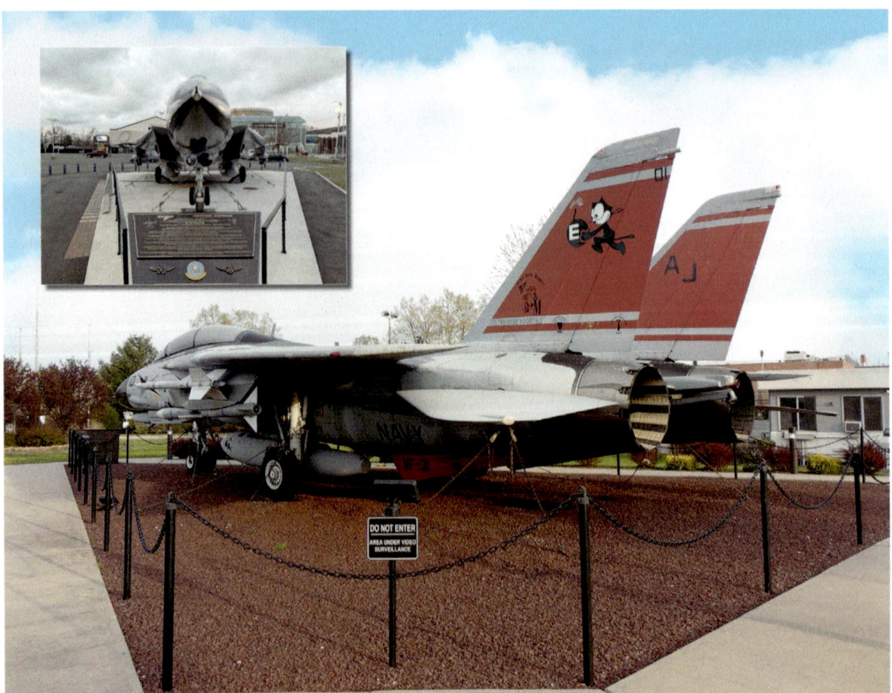

The last Grumman Tomcat to fly (2006) was on display at the Grumman property in Bethpage until it was moved in 2023 to the grounds of the Cradle of Aviation Museum in Garden City (inset).

parking lots, grass, and a water tower now sit where the main Grumman runway had once been. The most obvious sign of the area's past was the fierce-looking F-14 Tomcat fighter plane that until 2023 sat near the intersection of Grumman Road West and South Oyster Bay Road. F-14s were first flown in 1970; production on the plane ceased in 1992. The plane on display was number 711 of the 712 made, and was the last one to be flown, in 2006.

Sea Cliff Boardwalk Rebuilt (2007)

The north shore Nassau County village of Sea Cliff was founded as a religious retreat and soon became a pleasant summer resort filled with quaint and colorfully resplendent Victorian architecture, before settling into a year-round residential paradise and artist colony with its hundreds of vintage homes, scenic hilly streets, quaint shops and cafes, high cliffs, and beautiful waterfront views of the Long Island Sound. When a hurricane destroyed Sea Cliff's famous boardwalk in 1944, nobody realized it would take sixty-three years for it to be replaced. While residents still had a private beach to enjoy adjacent to the former site of the boardwalk, there was no sand-free (and Sea Cliff non-resident) option for taking in the vista. Finally, in 2007, a new 1,000-foot-long boardwalk was constructed at the base of Cliff Way at a cost of $1.6 million, allowing residents and visitors alike to once again enjoy the great views of the Long Island Sound, stroll, sit, or fish.

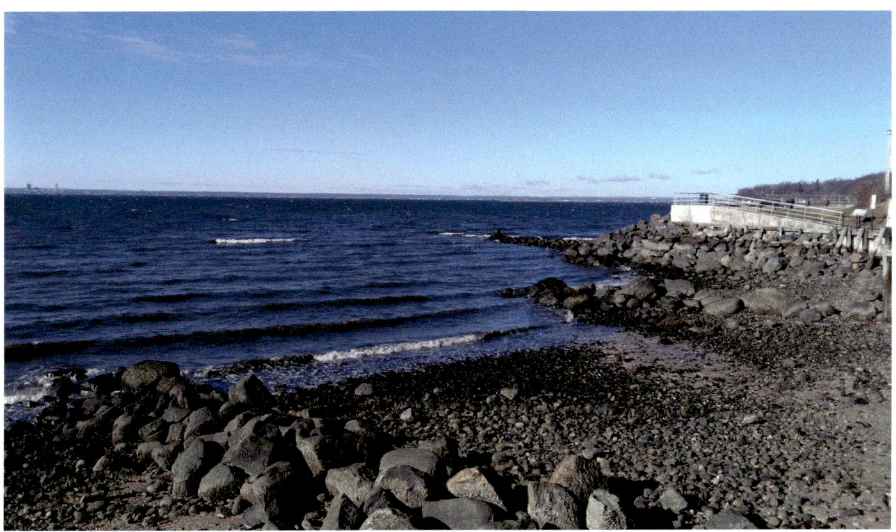

The view from the boardwalk at Sea Cliff along with part of the boardwalk (right center), as seen in 2018.

Long Island Hosts Presidential Debates (2008, 2012, 2016)

Every four years, voters get the chance to vote in the presidential election, and the debates that are held between the candidates become an important part of the decision-making process. Hempstead's Hofstra University hosted nationally televised presidential debates sponsored by the bipartisan Commission on Presidential Debates in 2008, 2012, and 2016—becoming the only university to host three consecutive presidential debates. On October 15, 2008, Hofstra hosted the final debate of the election season, between John McCain and Barack Obama (Obama won the election). On October 16, 2012, Hofstra hosted the second debate between Barack Obama and Mitt Romney (Obama won the election). Hofstra also hosted the contentious first debate of 2016 debate between Donald Trump and Hillary Clinton, on September 26 (Trump won the election). The 2016 Hofstra debate drew 84 million viewers, the most of any debate between 1960 and 2020. After leaving the debate stage, Clinton next made a brief stop at The Space in Westbury for a mini rally with her entourage. Among others, with her were former president Bill Clinton, then-governor Andrew Cuomo, and future governor Kathy Hochul.

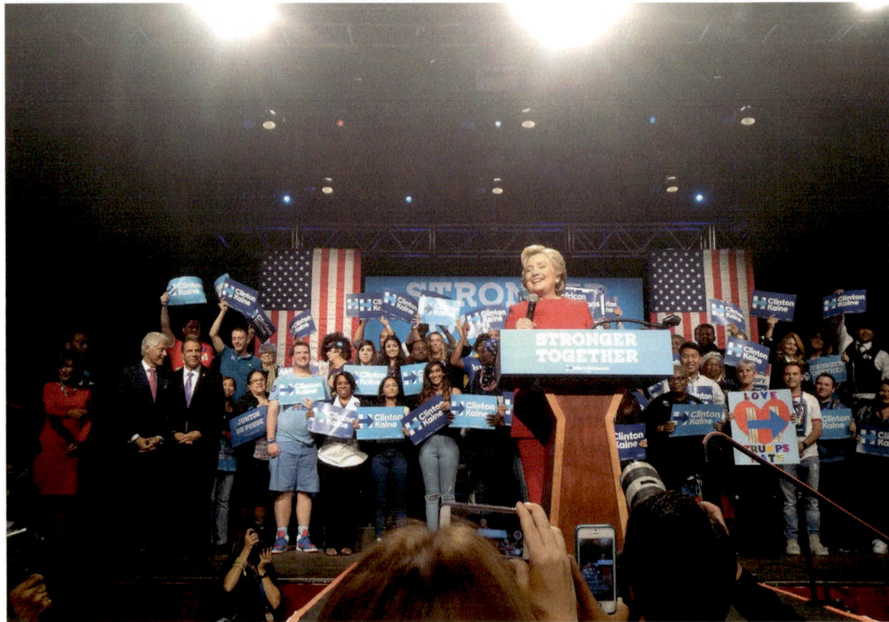

Hillary Clinton makes an appearance in Westbury following her October 2016 debate *versus* Donald Trump at Hofstra University. In the photo are also former president Bill Clinton, then-governor Andrew Cuomo, and future governor Kathy Hochul.

A Mall Dies and is Reborn (2009)

The Fortunoff department store had been a thriving fixture on Old Country Road in Westbury since 1964, and a major expansion at the site opened in September 1997. Now called the Mall at the Source, the 763,000-square-foot space had sixty-five stores or kiosks, including the 213,000-square-foot Fortunoff store. There was also a Virgin Megastore, a 375-seat Rainforest Café, and a spacious food court. Though it started strong, the mall did not attract enough customers. When the Rainforest Café closed in October 2000, it was already the fourth eatery to shutter. In 2009, both of the mall's anchor stores, Fortunoff and Circuit City, shuttered, setting off a domino effect. Stores and eateries began to close one after another—the bookstore, the toy store, the candle shop. Soon the mall was mostly empty, and by 2018, there was just a pet adoption center on the second floor. For several years, only Cheesecake Factory, P.F. Chang's, and Dave and Buster's remained with the rest of the mall consisting of empty corridors. The mall went into foreclosure in 2012, but an auction found no buyers to assume the $148 million in debt, so creditors took over. For a time in 2014 and 2015, there was speculation that the mall could become a casino, but that plan did not advance due to community opposition. By 2016, the mall was potentially slated to be demolished. Finally, in 2017, Lesso Mall Development Long Island Inc. bought the mall for $92 million, intending to reopen it as a mall of home improvement showrooms called Lesso Home New York in 2018, but the project was delayed. By 2019, the project had a new name: Samanea New York. The opening was delayed a few years, but finally new life began to appear in the space. By 2025, the revived mall contained a Fortunoff Backyard Store, the Empire Adventure Park, the Gravity Vault (rock climbing), Smash-It Pickleball and Smash-It Therapy, a couple of new restaurants, and a Ranch 99 Asian Market.

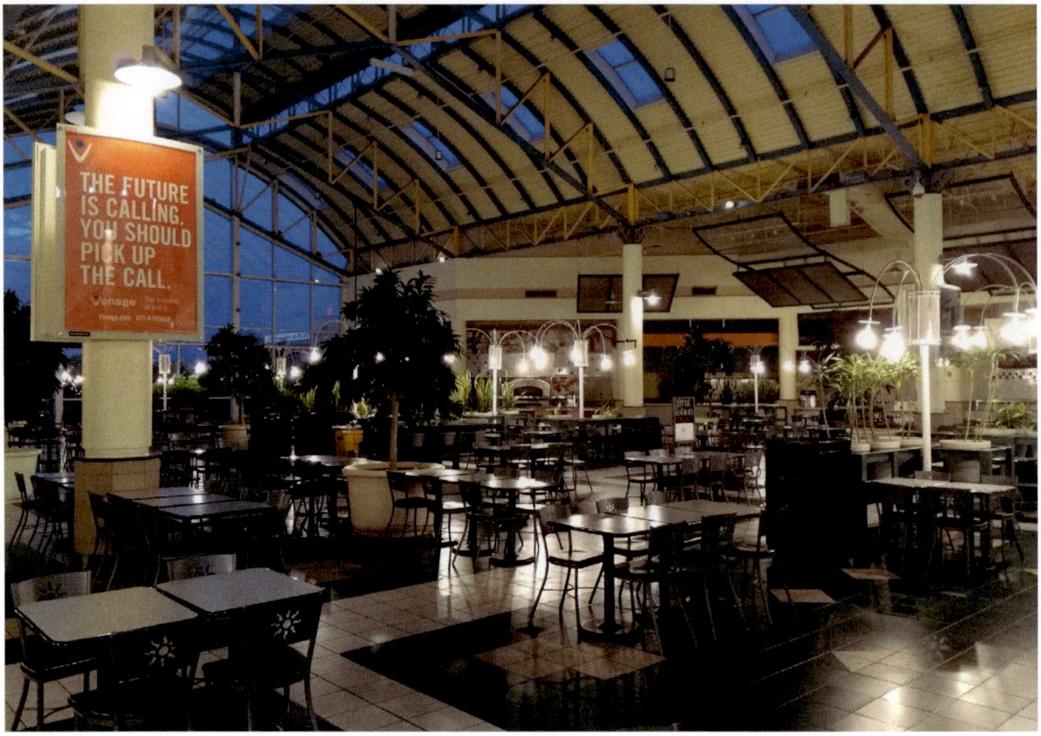

The empty food court at the Source Mall in Westbury as seen in 2017.

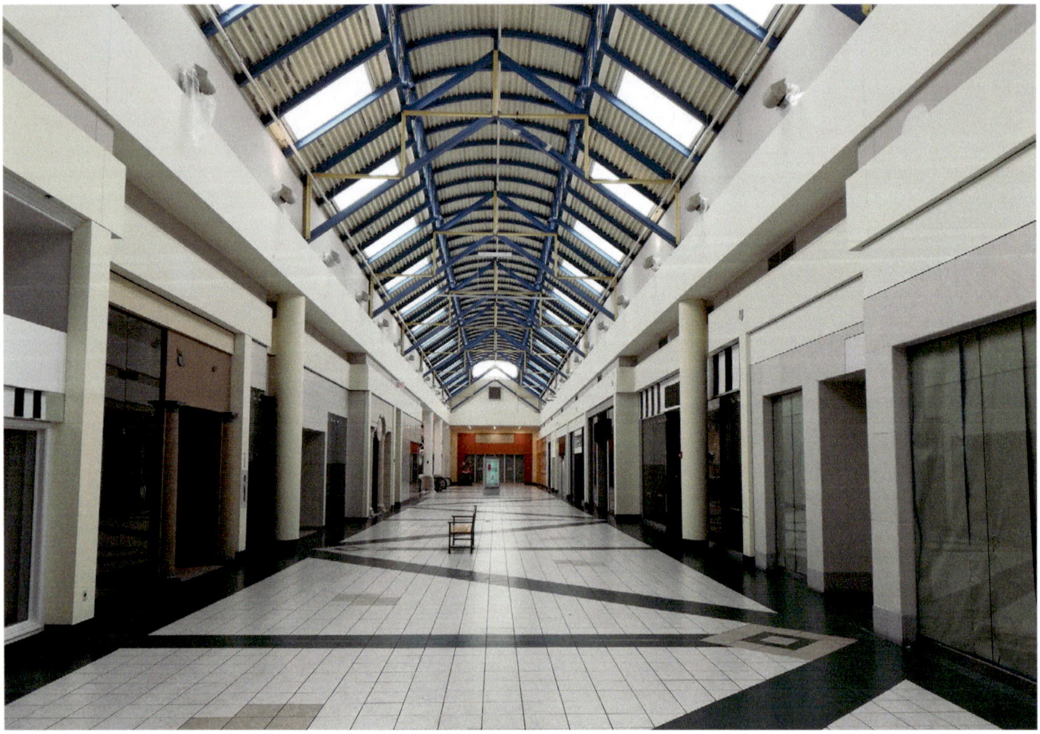

An empty corridor with closed stores at the Fortunoff Mall, 2019.

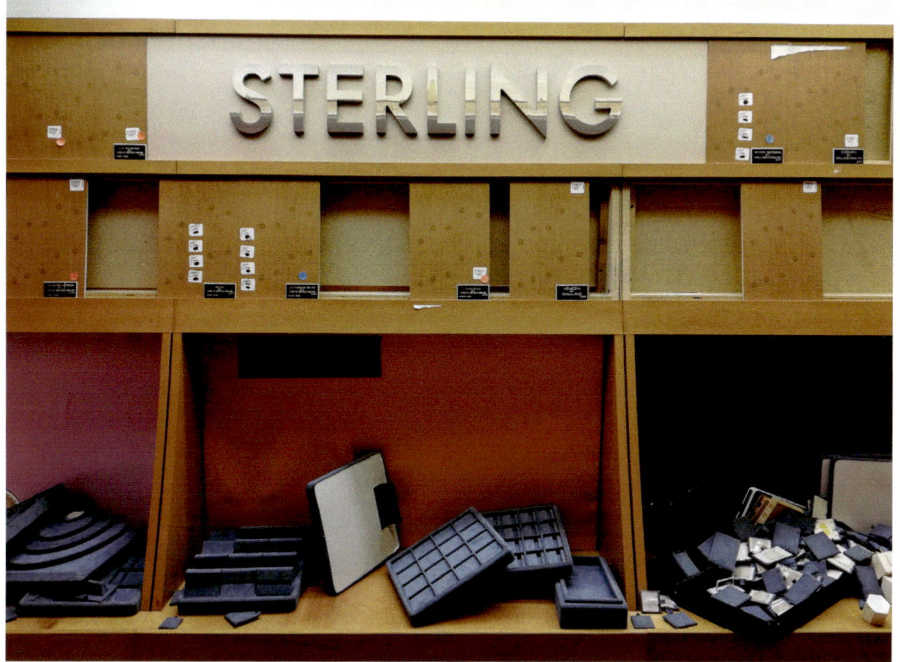

A jewelry display in the closed Fortunoff flagship store, 2019.

Gilgo Beach Murders (2010)

In December 2010, while searching for the body of missing escort Shannon Gilbert, who had called 911 from Oak Beach in May of that year, police found four sets of human remains on the marshy land just north of Ocean Parkway near Gilgo Beach in Suffolk County, a few miles east of Jones Beach. More remains were found nearby in 2011. Some of the victims had been missing as far back as the 1990s. Additional remains were found after that for a total of eleven victims (including Gilbert, whose remains were finally located), but for years there were no solid leads as to the perpetrator of these horrific crimes. A suspect in what was dubbed the Gilgo Beach serial killings was finally apprehended in July 2023, when an architect from Massapequa Park was arrested and charged with three murders; that number went up to six a few months later. He pleaded not guilty. The suspect was apprehended based on his car being spotted at the home of one of the victims. The victims were Craigslist escorts that the suspect allegedly met and then killed and dismembered. In 2024, he was indicted on additional murder charges. In late 2024, his estranged wife announced she was moving out of their longtime Massapequa Park home. The suspect's attorney sought a change in venue for the trial, with the belief that his client would not be able to get a fair trial in Suffolk County.

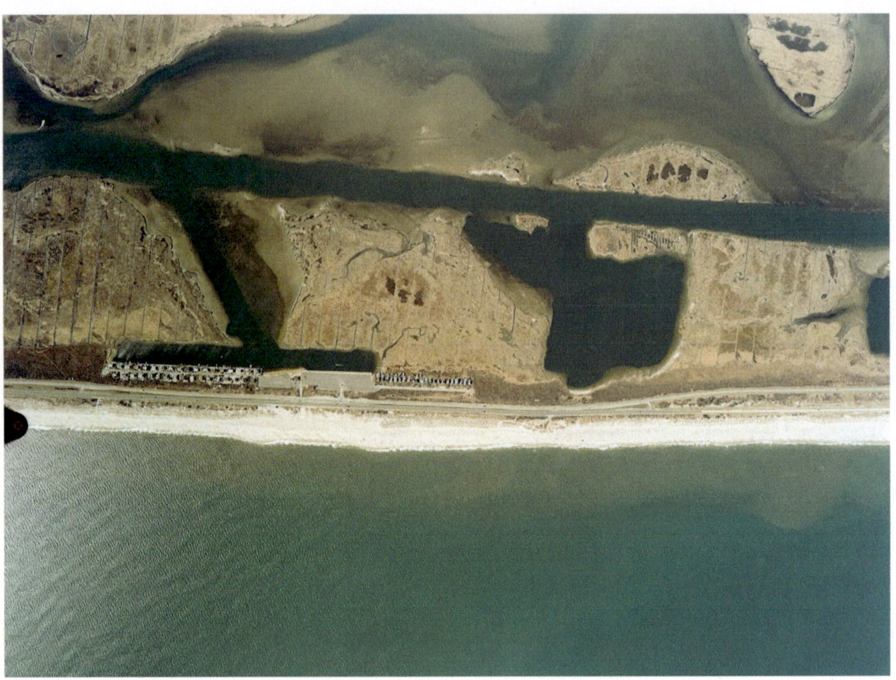

An aerial view of the Gilgo Beach site where several murder victims' remains were found in 2010 and 2011.

Billy's Bikes (2010)

Long Island native Billy Joel has long had an obsession with motorcycles. In 2010, he opened up a business on Audrey Avenue in his beloved Oyster Bay (near to his then-home in Centre Island) called 20th Century Cycles. A combination repair/restoration shop and a museum and storage space for his collection, it is open to the public on weekends and features some very cool memorabilia (such as a sign noting a landmark concert at Madison Square Garden) as well as a carefully curated display of his seventy-five-plus vintage motorbikes as well as occasional automobiles. According to Joel, he likes the old-fashioned aesthetic of bikes and cars from the '30s to the '60s and wanted to have a display to show off that classic style. Mechanics work on restoring and repairing and maintaining his collection, to which he has added over the years; the displays change regularly. T-shirts and other small souvenirs are for sale at 20th Century Cycles, but the bikes themselves are not. In 2024, Joel put his 26-acre Centre Island property up for sale for $49.9 million, wanting to spend more time in Florida (though still retaining a smaller property elsewhere on Long Island).

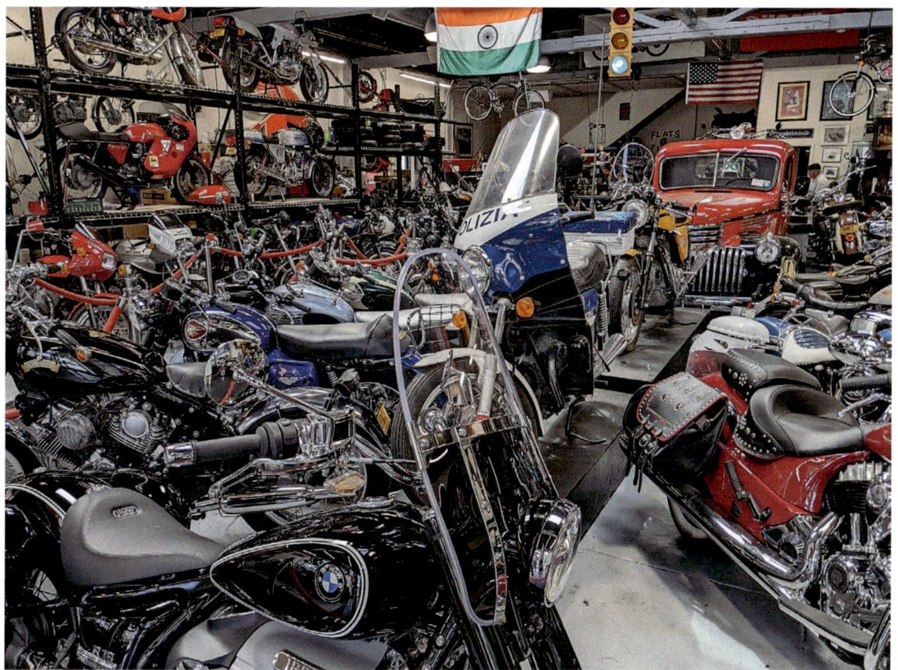

Inside 20th Century Cycles, the motorcycle museum/repair shop in Oyster Bay owned by Billy Joel, seen here in 2022. The displays change as Joel purchases new bikes (and sometimes sports cars as well).

New Concert Venues (2011)

Long Island has a long history of live music. Some of the biggest acts of the '70s, '80s, and '90s appeared at venues ranging from Nassau Coliseum (featuring memorable shows by major artists such as Elvis Presley, Led Zeppelin, Pink Floyd, and the Jacksons) in Uniondale to the intimate My Father's Place venue in Rosyln (which gave a stage to up-and-coming acts such as the Ramones, Billy Joel, and the Talking Heads). By 2000, the best of the Coliseum's days were behind it, and My Father's Place had long since been shuttered. However, the music scene on Long Island has enjoyed a revival in recent years. Several new musical venues opened in the opening years of the twenty-first century, bringing a whole new range of big musical names—past and present—to Long Island. In 2018, My Father's Place found a new home at the Roslyn Hotel after holding some shows at temporary locations in the area; their 2024 events included a show by '70s star Al Stewart and '80s star Midge Ure. Meanwhile, the Paramount Theater on New York Avenue in Huntington (opened in 2011 in the former space of the IMAX Theater) quickly became immensely popular and has attracted some major stars. In 2022, Pollstar named it the best club venue in the world, ranked by ticket sales. The Space in Westbury on Post Avenue (opened in 2013) was also a 1920s movie theater that was successfully converted into an intimate concert venue. The venue that had long been known as the Westbury Music Fair finally got back part of its name in 2024, when it was renamed Flagstar at Westbury Music Fair. Meanwhile, out east, the Suffolk Theater in Riverhead reopened as a concert venue in 2013, offering great live shows and dinner. Acts there have included The Lords of 52nd Street, Billy Joel's original backing band.

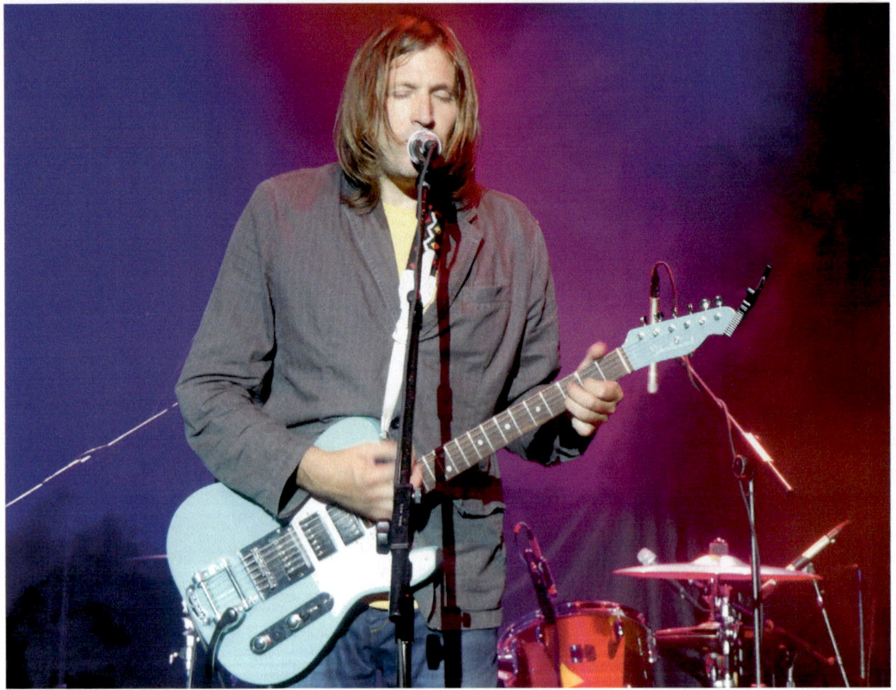

Evan Dando of Soul Asylum performs at the recently opened Space at Westbury theater in 2013.

Opposite above: A 2024 concert at the Paramount in Huntington, one of the top venues in the country.

Opposite below: The Long Island Music Hall of Fame is also a concert venue, frequently hosting local musicians on its stage. In this photo, a band takes the stage in November 2024.

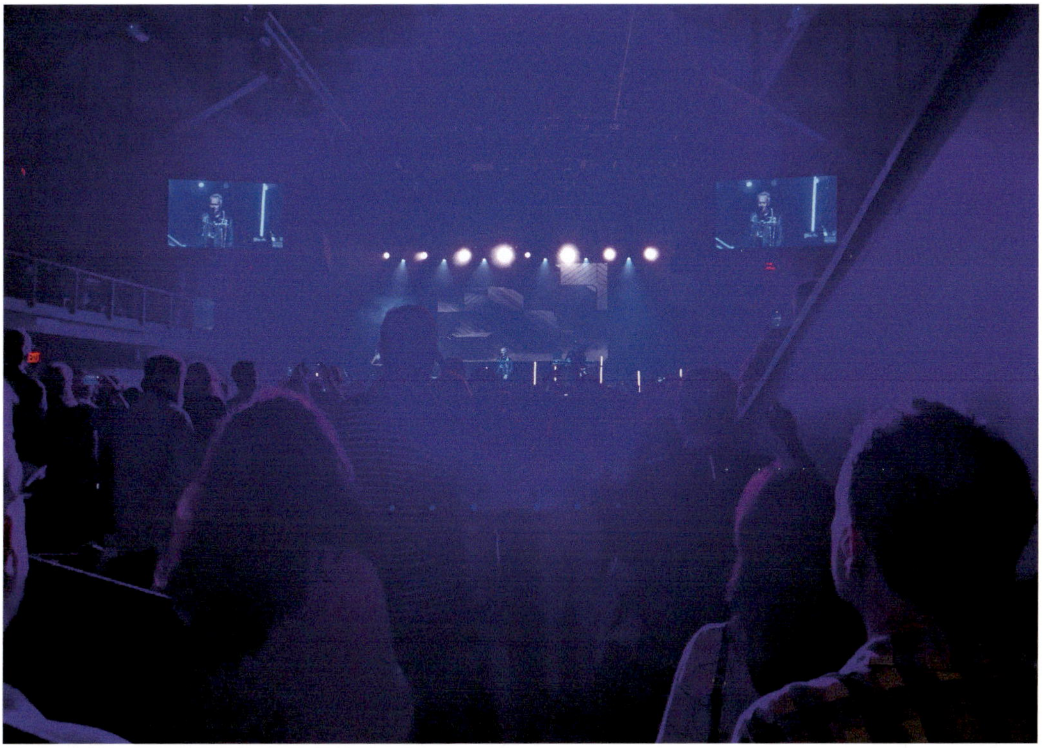

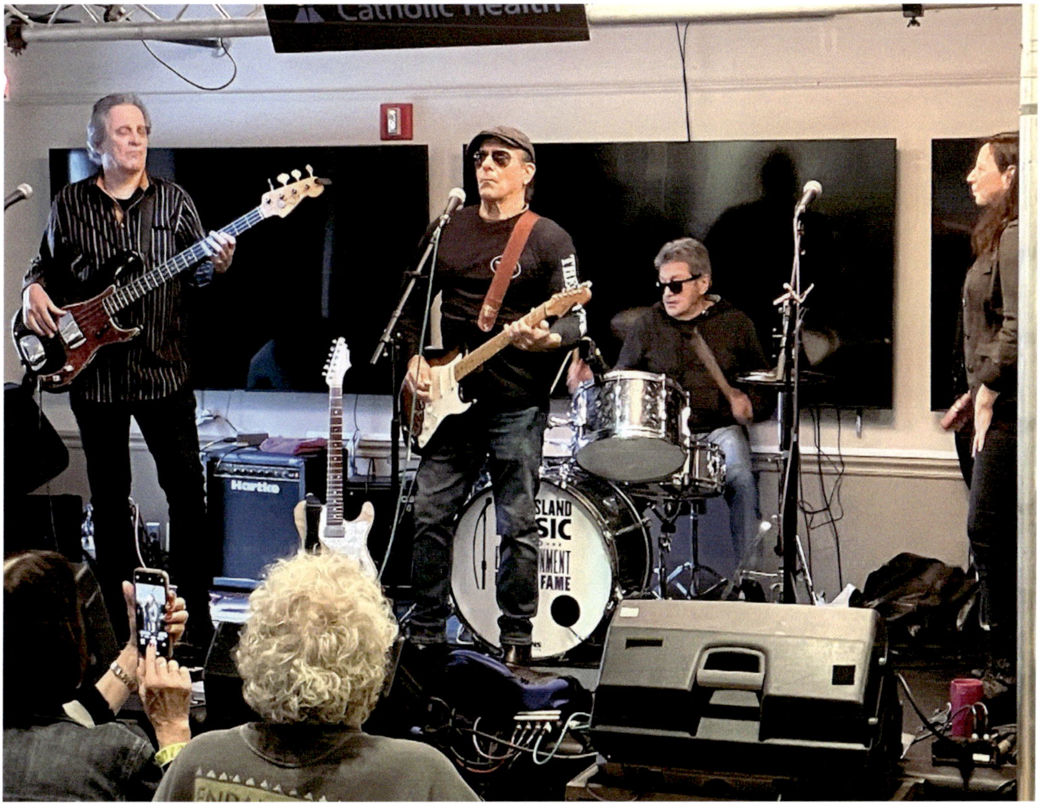

New Supermarkets (2011)

Some of the earliest supermarkets on Long Island included Bohack's, A&P, Waldbaum's, and King Kullen (acknowledged by the Smithsonian as America's first supermarket; the first store opened in Jamaica in 1930). Some of these early supermarkets of the 1940s and '50s were located in village downtowns while others catered to the suburbia that Long Island was becoming, opening in locations on busy roads such as Old Country Road and Jericho Turnpike. Later additions to the Long Island food shopping experience included Queens-based Western Beef, Massachusetts-based Stop & Shop, New Jersey-based Shoprite, and superstores such as Walmart, BJ's, and Costco. Target opened its first Long Island stores in 1998, becoming another popular grocery option. In the twenty-first century, a new round of stores debuted on the island to compete with the existing options. Aldi (first LI store in Bay Shore in 2011, thirteen locations as of 2024) and Lidl (first LI stores in Center Moriches and West Babylon in 2019, twenty-five locations as of 2024) were both German-owned companies known for their low prices and interesting selection of products (including of course, German-made items). In 2016, Connecticut-based Stew Leonard's (famous for its maze-like store setup and animatronic singing displays) opened in Farmingdale and in 2017, a store in East Meadow. And in 2024, Rochester-based Wegmans began hiring for its first Long Island location in Lake Grove which opened in early 2025.

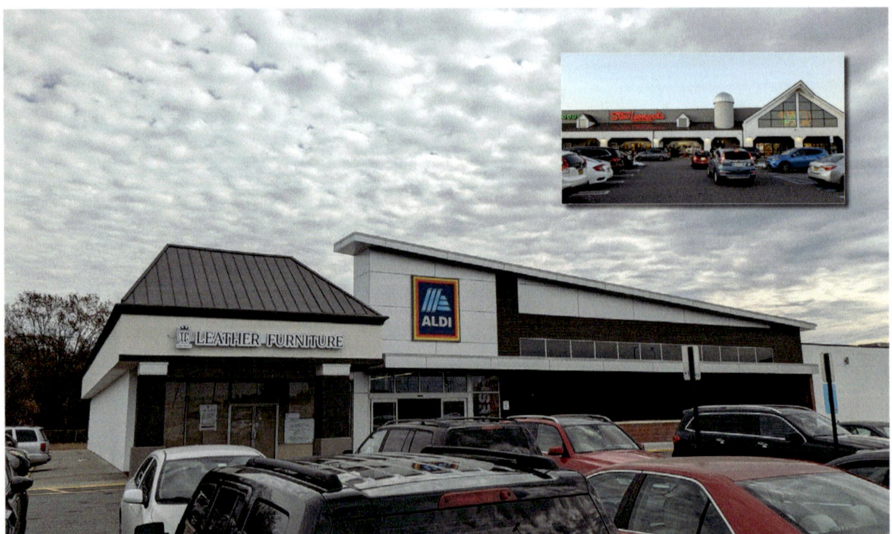

Many new supermarkets opened on Long Island in the first quarter of the twenty-first century, including Aldi and Stew Leonard's (inset).

That Bus is NICE (2012)

In 1973, Nassau County's complicated bus system, at the time comprised of ten separate private bus operating companies, was taken over by a wholly owned subsidiary of the Metropolitan Transportation Authority (MTA). By 2010, however, the MTA was threatening to cut service due to the county's inability to pay its share of the costs. In 2011, the MTA voted to stop all service in Nassau County by the beginning of 2012. The county contracted with a private company called Veolia Transport (now called Transdev) to operate the bus system, which was to be renamed Nassau Inter-County Express (NICE). The distinctive orange buses can be seen across forty-one routes throughout the county, carrying about 80,000 passengers daily. Many routes originate in the hub of Hempstead. As of 2025, bus fare was $2.90 ($1.45 for seniors), and the system had 850 employees and offered 300,000 trips per year using a fleet of over 280 fixed route buses and 100 paratransit vehicles.

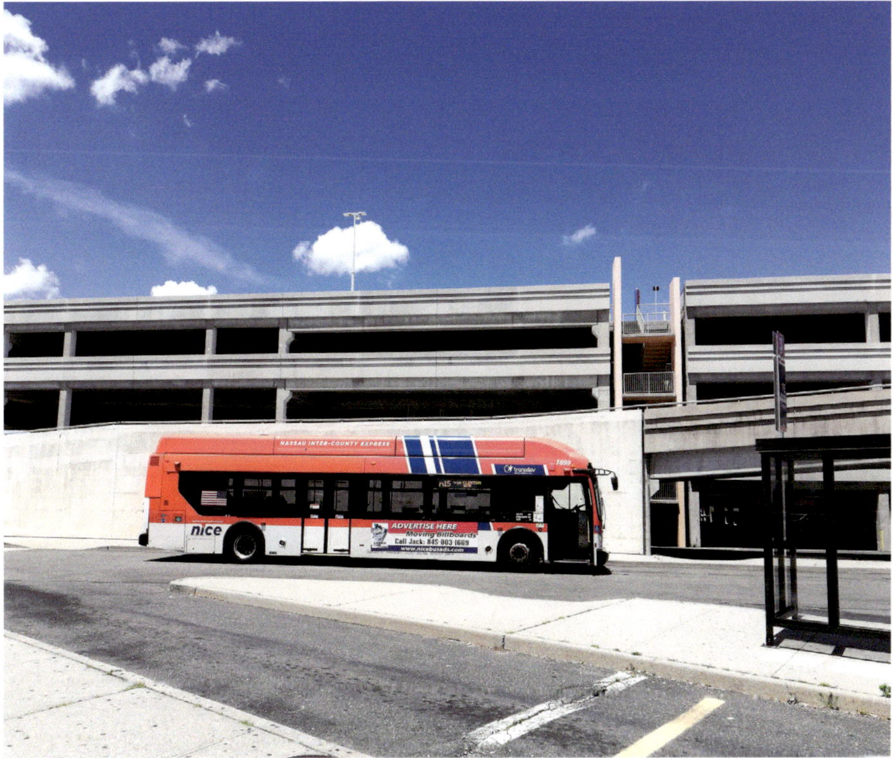

The distinctive orange and blue Nassau Inter-County Express (NICE) buses can be seen traversing many county roads day and night, carrying passengers to locations including the Roosevelt Field Mall, as seen in this 2020 photo.

Hurricane Sandy (2012)

On October 29, 2012, an Atlantic hurricane-turned-superstorm named Sandy ravaged coastal Long Island (especially the ocean-facing south shore), wrecking parts of Jones Beach, Atlantic Beach, and Long Beach and destroying property from the Rockaways to Montauk. Its primary effect was storm surge; in many locations the water rose above the FEMA 100-year base flood elevation, inundating streets, homes, and businesses. In addition, its winds were powerful enough to down countless trees and cause power outages to 900,000 customers across the island. For many of us, it took days to restore the power, as trees first had to be cut and removed before the power lines could be repaired. Over 95,000 Long Island buildings were damaged or destroyed by the storm. A months-long damage control effort was quickly begun to rehabilitate, restore, and replace the hardest-hit damaged areas, including Jones Beach and Freeport. Waterfront homes and businesses were repaired and streets and boardwalks were repaired or replaced. In the process, tons of sand and debris were removed. Since then, major coastal infrastructure improvement programs were implemented in New York City and on Long Island's south shore to provide more protection against future storm events at a time when climate change and rising sea levels could mean more frequent flooding and more intense storms. The Army Corps of Engineers led a $125 million project in Long Beach that included placing over 4 million cubic yards of sand, while the Fire Island to Moriches Inlet saw a $291 million restoration effort that placed 7 million cubic yards of sand to restore the dunes. A massive Fire Island to Montauk Point project valued at $1.8 billion includes beach nourishment, home elevations, flood-proofing measures, and a breach response plan.

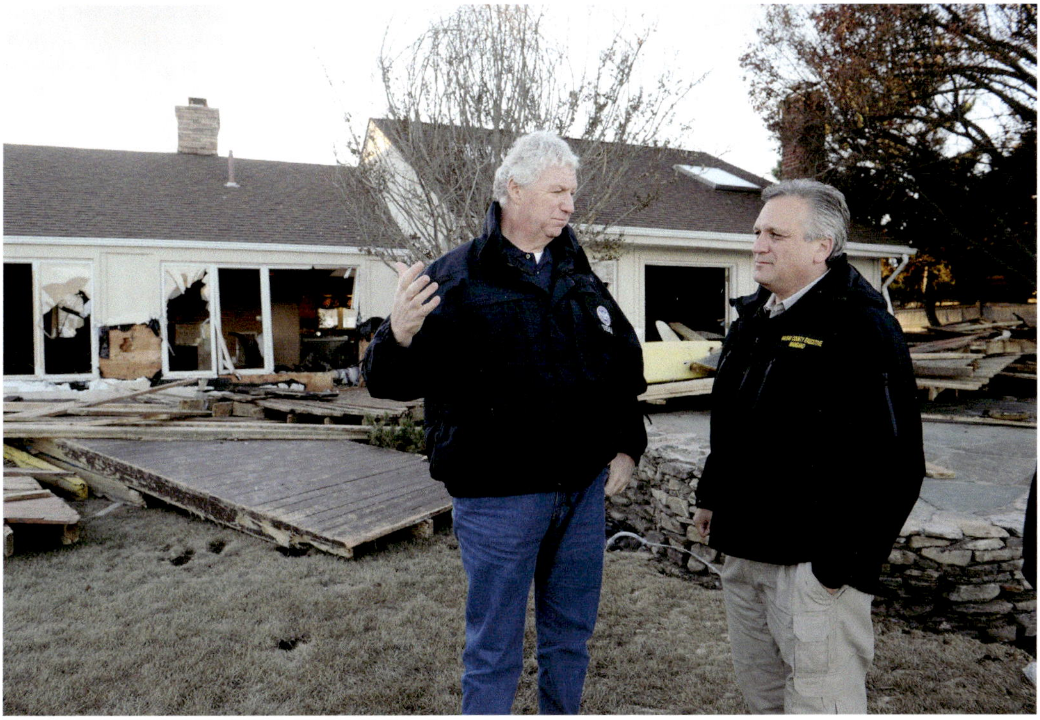

FEMA Deputy Administrator Rich Serino (left) and County Executive Edmund Mangano visit Massapequa, an area heavily impacted by Hurricane Sandy, on November 6, 2012.

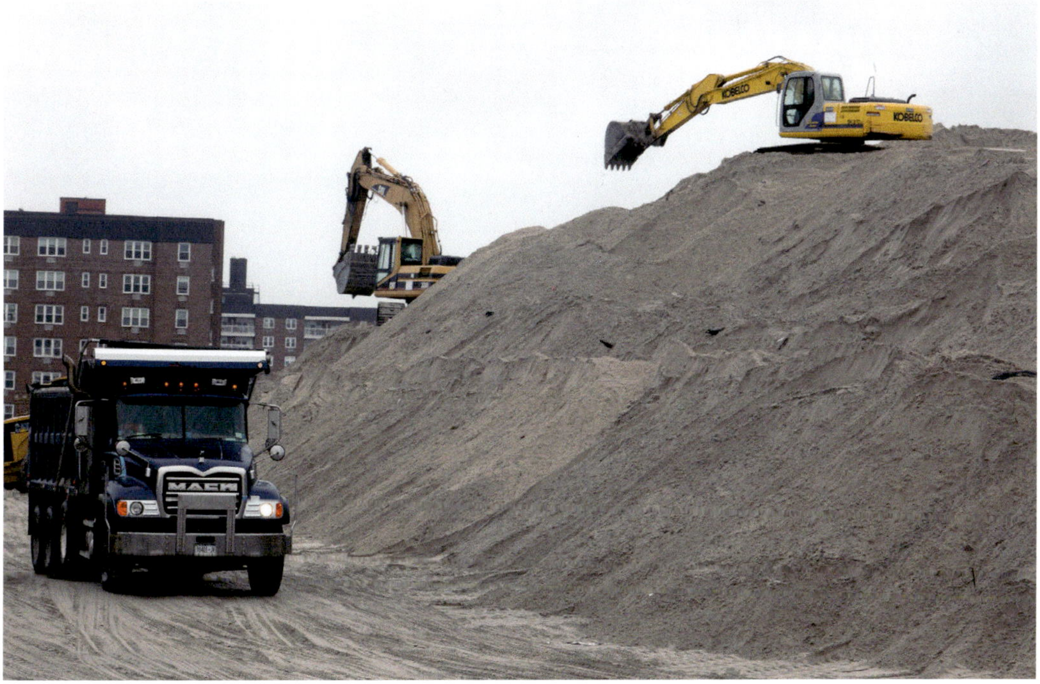

A mountain of sand piled up from the streets of Long Beach after a storm surge from Hurricane Sandy swept through the town, November 7, 2012.

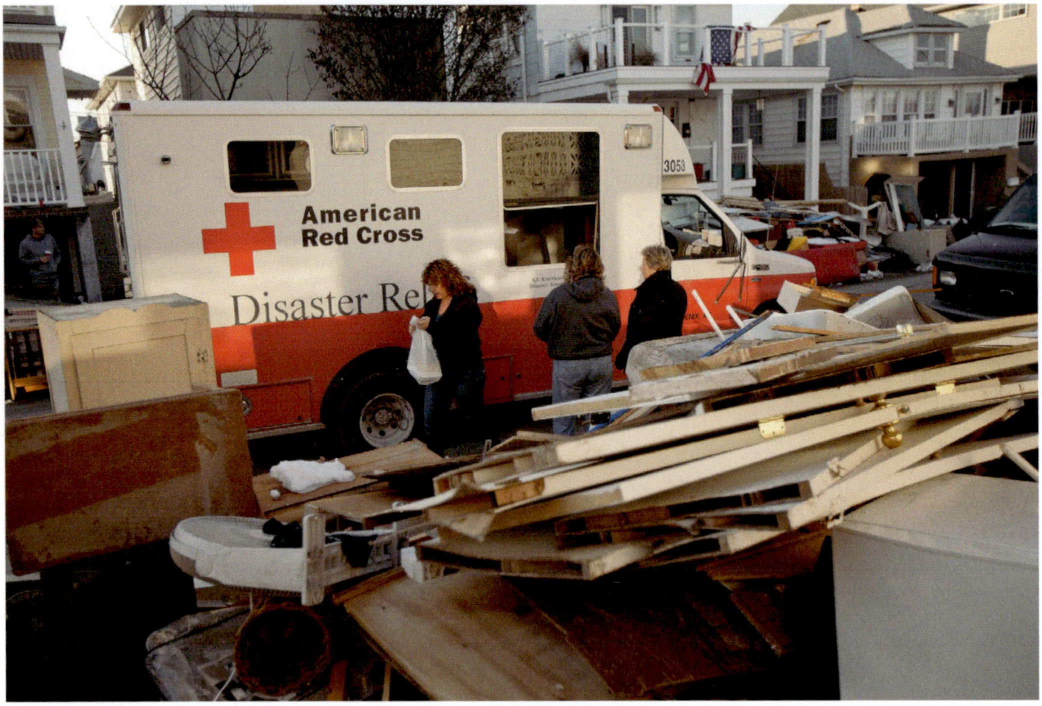

Debris piled high outside of Long Beach homes on November 9, 2012. Hurricane Sandy created widespread flooding, power outages, and devastation across Long Island. The Federal Emergency Management Agency (FEMA) worked with state and local officials to assist residents who were affected by the hurricane.

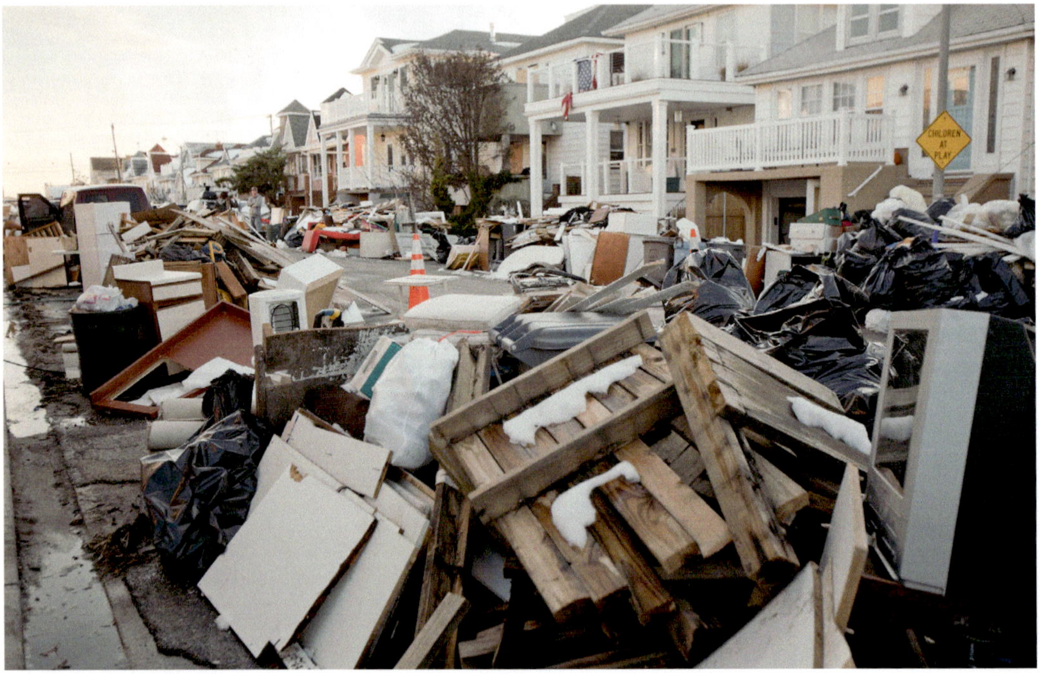

The American Red Cross delivers food to Hurricane Sandy survivors in a Long Island neighborhood on November 9, 2012. The hurricane created widespread flooding, power outages, and devastation to the area.

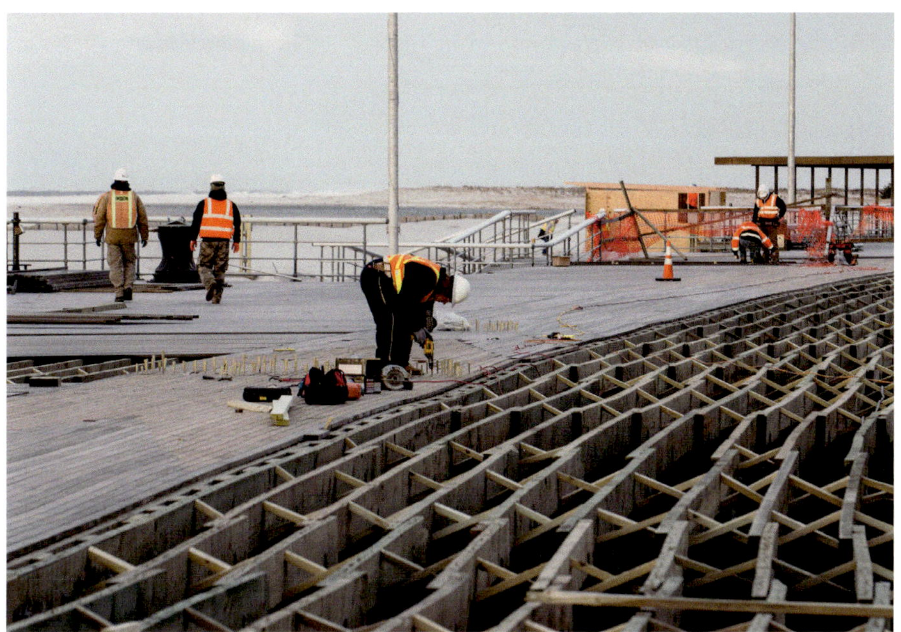

The New York State Office of Parks, Recreation & Historic Preservation received $2.4 million in funding from FEMA for repairs to the 2-mile Jones Beach boardwalk (shown in March 2013). Work proceeded through the winter of 2012–13 to repair the heavily damaged boardwalk to get it ready for the summer season. The boardwalk officially reopened on Memorial Day weekend, 2013.

Roslyn Viaduct is Replaced (2012)

The original pin-and-hanger structure spanning over Roslyn Harbor (carrying Route 25A) was built in 1949 as a bypass for vehicles crossing east-west through Roslyn so they did not have to drive through the center of the quaint village and cause traffic congestion. By the turn of the twenty-first century, the old viaduct was showing its age and there was extra concern because its structure type was unfortunately similar to that of the Mianus River Bridge carrying I-95 in Connecticut, a bridge that collapsed in 1983. Safety concerns led to the State Department of Transportation commissioning the design of a new structure during the 1990s; construction began in 2006 and was completed in phases to mitigate traffic impacts. The north half of the old bridge was demolished and reconstructed first while all traffic was rerouted to the existing southern half. The new northern half opened to traffic in 2009 and work began on the southern half. The new 2,200-foot-long structure, officially renamed the William Cullen Bryant Viaduct after the famous nineteenth-century poet, editor, and Rosyln resident, carries about 31,000 vehicles daily. It is a precast concrete segmental bridge (the first in New York State) whose segments were erected and connected together like puzzle pieces.

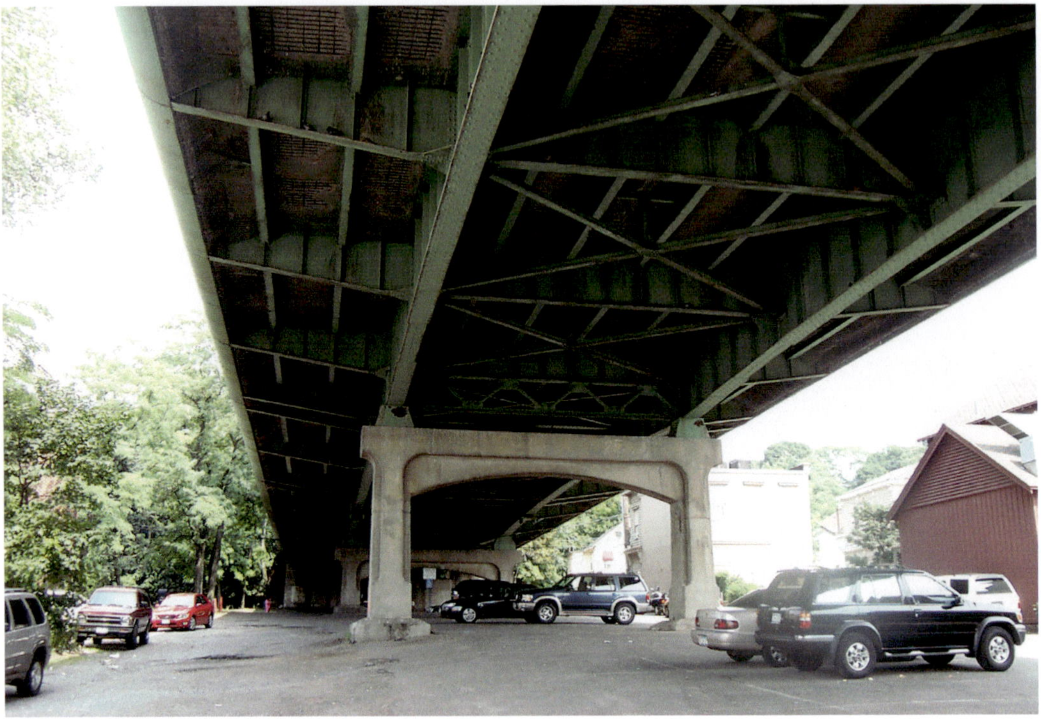

The original Roslyn Viaduct was demolished and replaced starting in 2006. Its structure type was seen as obsolete and unsafe.

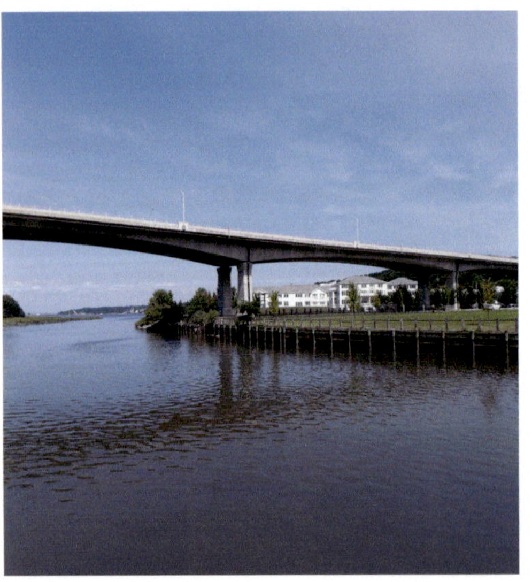

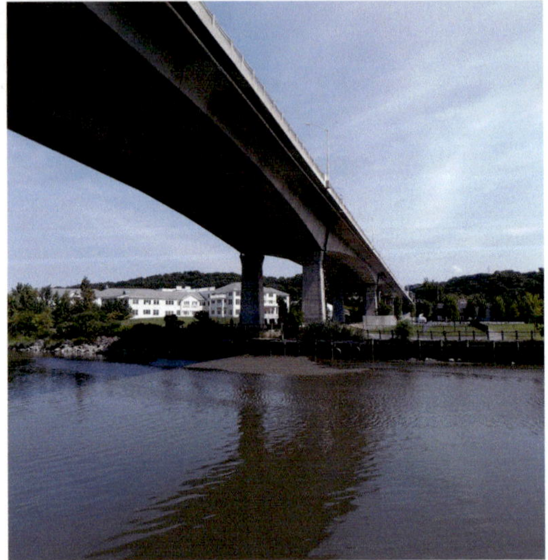

The new Roslyn Viaduct, aka the William Cullen Bryant Viaduct, seen here in 2017, was New York State's first precast concrete segmental bridge.

"Blank Space" Video is Filmed (2014)

In October 2014, Taylor Swift released her fourth album, *1989* (named after her birth year). Already a global superstar by then, she had recently made the full-on transition from country-tinged music to pop. One of the biggest tracks on the new album was "Blank Space," a song about a woman who cycles through a lot of men, singing that she has a "blank space" in which to write their names. The iconic video for this song contributed to its overall popularity. Filmed over three days in September 2014, at the 1920s Huntington estate known as Oheka Castle (now home to a lavish hotel and restaurant), it made excellent use of the beautiful gardens to provide a lush, lavish backdrop for Taylor and her on-screen boyfriend Sean O'Pry (also born 1989). The couple seems happy during the first half of the video, but then Taylor gets jealous and wreaks havoc on her boyfriend's shirts, and the portrait she'd painted of him. Two classic cars were featured in the video—a silver Shelby Cobra (a 2008 reproduction) and a red 1957 Jaguar XK 150 convertible. An angry Swift takes a golf club to the Shelby toward the end of the video, which as of 2025 had over 3.6 billion views. In an interesting coincidence, the video was directed by Joseph Kahn and the Oheka Castle was originally Otto Kahn's estate (no relation;

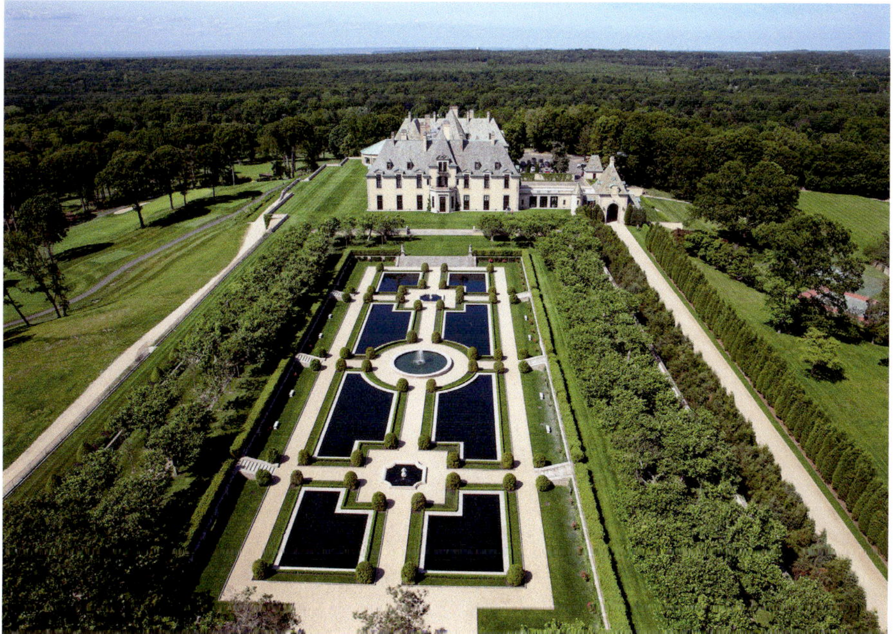

Oheka Castle, part of the Otto Kahn estate, was built in the 1920s and was one of the largest mansions in the country. In 2014, Taylor Swift filmed the video for the massive hit song "Blank Space" here.

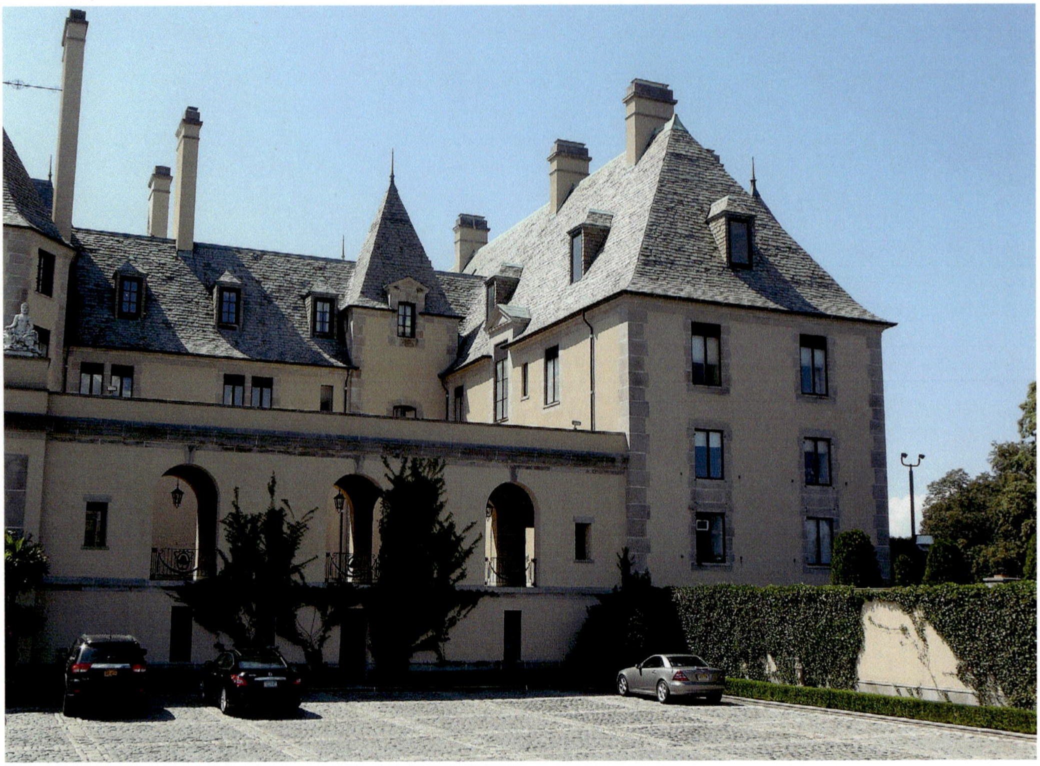

Above and below: A close-up view of the Oheka Castle mansion in 2014. Taylor Swift filmed parts of the video right outside the building and on the beautifully landscaped grounds.

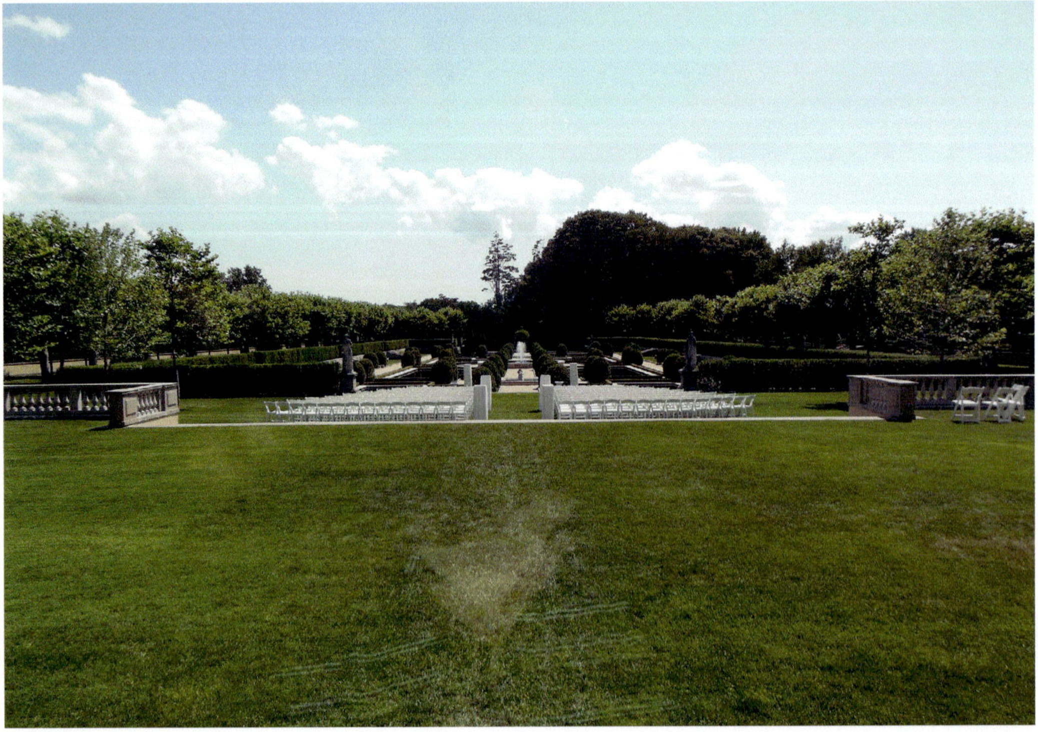

Joseph is South Korean). Interior shots were filmed at another Long Island Gold Coast estate—Winfield Hall in Glen Cove (aka the Woolworth estate). The "Blank Space" video was not the only time Taylor Swift set foot on Long Island; she has been a frequent visitor over the years. In 2014, she visited her friend Ina Garten in East Hampton for a cooking photo shoot and later that year had dinner with director Steven Spielberg in East Hampton. In 2015, she filmed a Keds sneakers commercial in Montauk, and in 2016 she attended a birthday party in the Hamptons where she joined singer Nelly performing his 2002 song "Dilemma."

Long Island Motor Parkway Trail (2014)

The Long Island Motor Parkway (aka Vanderbilt Motor Parkway) was the world's first limited-access concrete highway. Devised by automobile enthusiast William Kissam Vanderbilt Jr. (1878–1944), work on the parkway began in 1908, with 9 miles of roadway from Westbury to Bethpage. The new highway was completely grade separated from other existing roads and railroad tracks. There were sixty-five bridges carrying the parkway and over the parkway along the route. By 1910, the parkway extended from Mineola to Lake Ronkonkoma. Additional segments followed in Queens, and by 1926, it had reached its westernmost point in Fresh Meadows. Though innovative for its time, Long Island had outgrown the narrow, curvy toll road by the 1930s. The construction of the Northern State Parkway sealed its fate. The old highway was decommissioned and sold to New York State for $80,000 in 1938 and much of it was demolished with the original highway property being used as right-of-way for power lines. A stretch of parkway, however, was preserved in Queens as a walking and biking path through Alley Pond/Cunningham Parks. There has been talk of creating a multi-use trail further east that followed the old Motor Parkway right-of-way as much as possible; finally in 2014, Nassau County completed construction of a 1-mile demonstration segment, on Salisbury Park Drive (adjacent to Eisenhower Park), from Carman Avenue to Stewart Avenue, using money from a remaining environmental bond act allocation. The overall trail plan includes eight segments in total. A 2.2-mile segment connecting with the existing Bethpage State Parkway and extending eastward to Old Bethpage Village Restoration and the Nassau Suffolk border via Spagnoli Road is in the state's budget plan for construction in 2026.

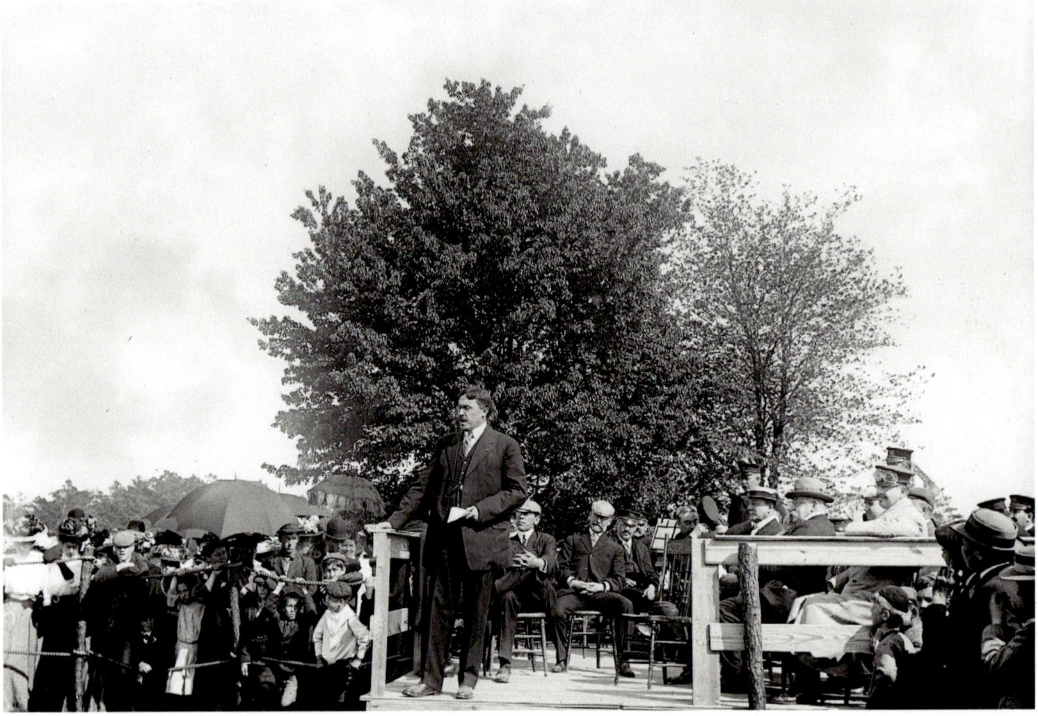

The dedication ceremony for the Long Island Motor Parkway, June 1908, in Bethpage. The parkway was the world's first modern highway, but it became obsolete within thirty years and was closed in 1938.

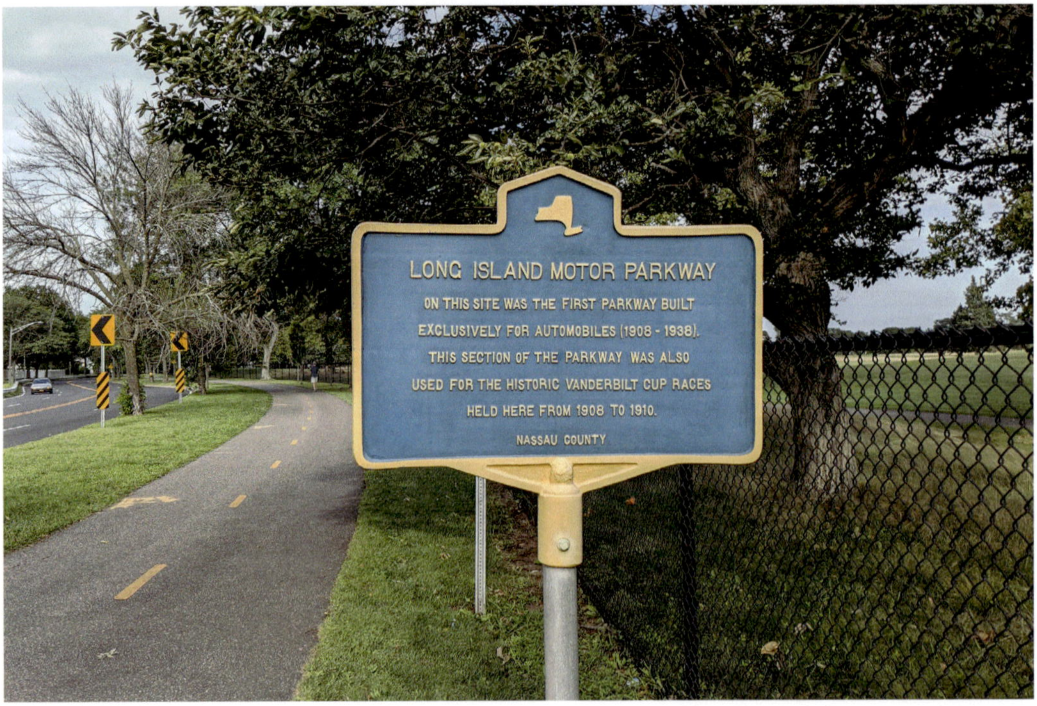

A historical marker commemorates where the parkway crossed through what is now Eisenhower Park.

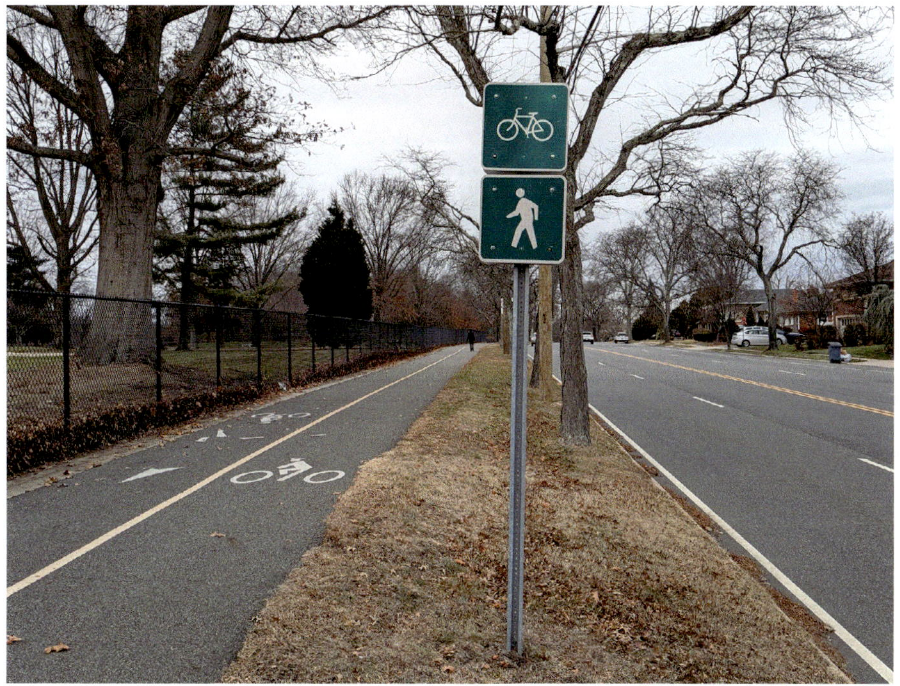

The first segment of the Long Island Motor Parkway Trail was opened in 2014 along Salisbury Park Drive adjacent to the east side of Eisenhower Park.

A New Cemetery (2016)

Polo was an immensely popular sport during the Gold Coast era on Long Island during the early twentieth century, and Old Westbury resident Tommy Hitchcock, Jr., was known as the Babe Ruth of polo. At an early age, he displayed rare talent and became an internationally known star. F. Scott Fitzgerald even based his character Tom Buchanan, in *The Great Gatsby*, on Hitchcock. The polo star grew up on a large property just north of Jericho Turnpike. After it left family control, it was in private hands until the 1990s when a drug bust resulted in the property being seized by the federal government. It was sold at auction in 1995 to the Diocese of Rockville Centre, which intended to turn the land into a cemetery because its other property, Holy Rood Cemetery in Westbury, was close to full. The new cemetery was rejected by the Village of Old Westbury on account of traffic, property value, and zoning concerns. Thus began an epic battle that lasted over twenty years, with lawsuits filed, zoning laws were picked apart, and demands made. The lawsuit was settled, and the cemetery was finally given a green light in 2016. Queen of Peace Cemetery finally opened and saw its first interment in May 2020, with a potential for up to 200,000 burials. The cemetery chapel features two distinctive 65-foot-high steeples.

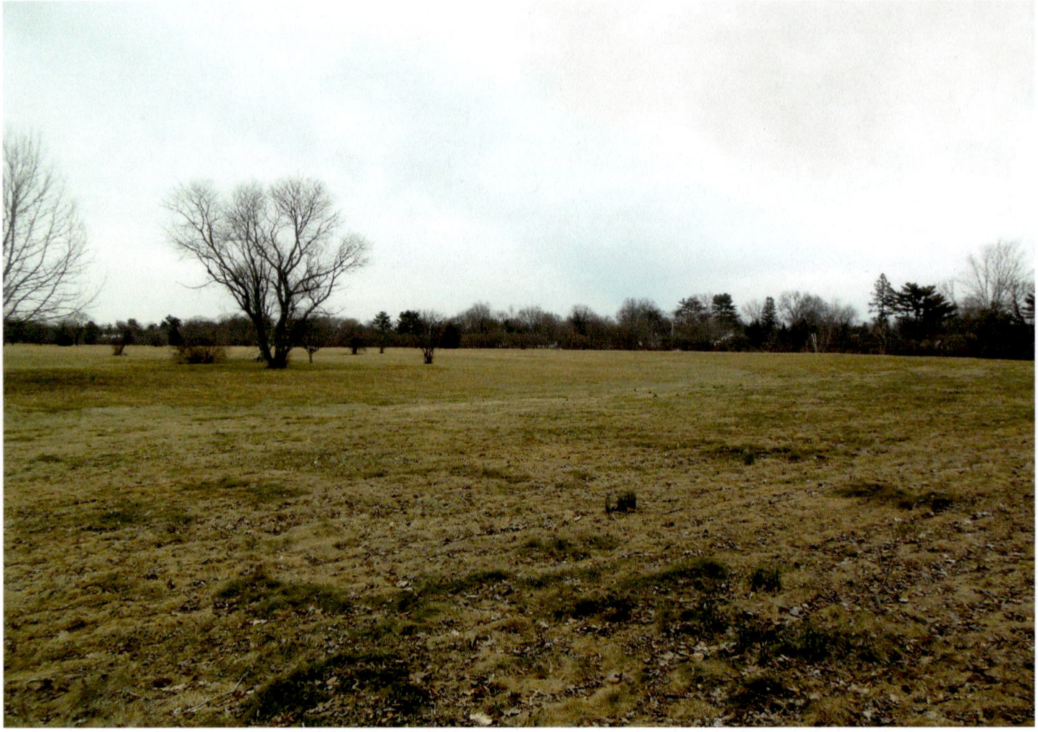

The Queen of Peace Cemetery in Old Westbury was formerly the Thomas Hitchcock estate. Hitchcock was a famous polo player. This 2016 image shows a field on the estate that was once home to a horse racing track.

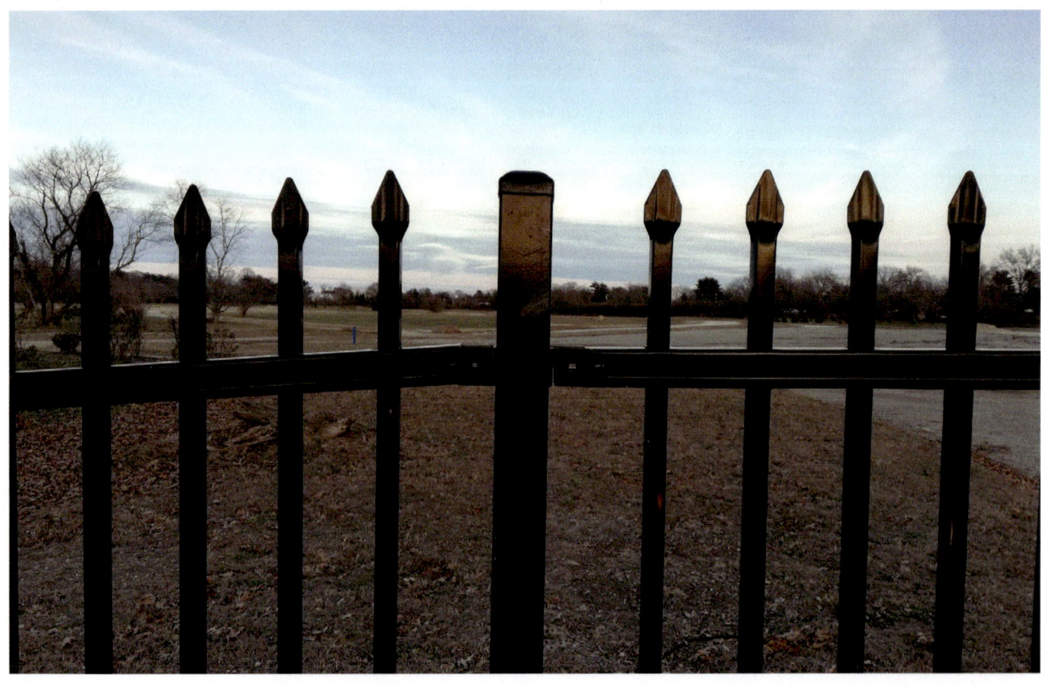

Construction of the cemetery finally began after years of legal wrangling. This 2019 photo shows the work in progress as seen from a gate on Hitchcock Lane.

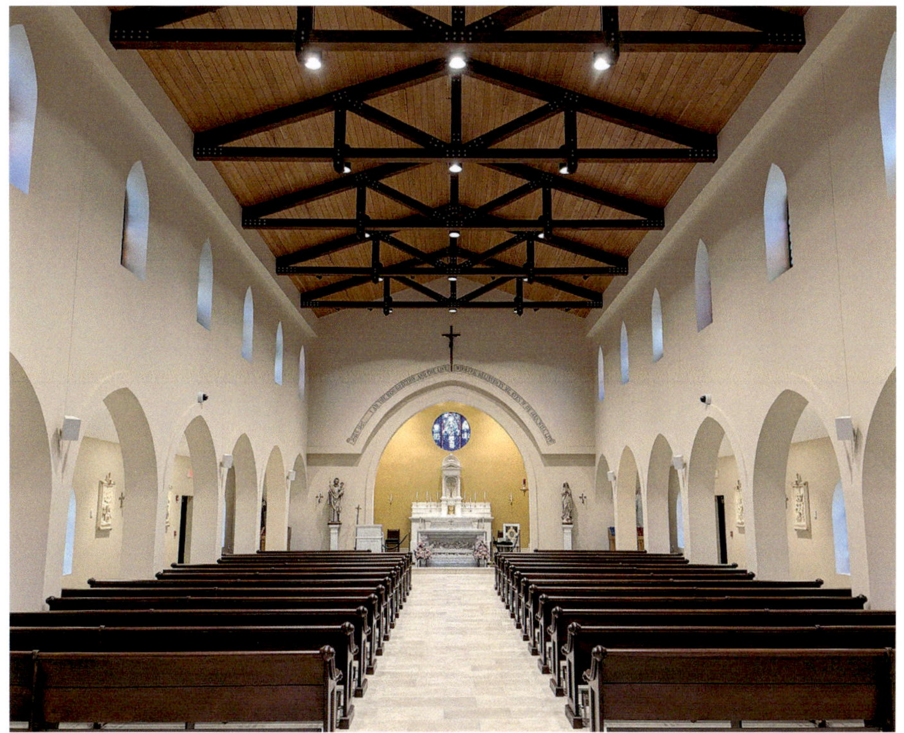

The cemetery includes a new chapel that can rival many of Long Island's finest churches for its design and spaciousness.

Downtown Revivals (2016)

Once thriving and bustling village centers, by the late twentieth century, many Long Island downtowns were suffering from neglect and high vacancy rates as automobile-accessible retail opened along popular routes such as Old Country Road, Jericho Turnpike, Hempstead Turnpike, Sunrise Highway, and others. These locations were sometimes miles away from the traditional downtown, drawing customers away from Main Street. Small, independent drugstores, variety stores, and hardware stores (among others) lost out to the "big box" and chain stores that spread across the island. Thankfully, the trend started to reverse as we welcomed the twenty-first century. The importance of a thriving Main Street was recognized, and state and federally funded revitalization grants led to villages across the island trying to rejuvenate their downtowns and bring shoppers back. It also led to new housing units being built by the thousands to accommodate smart growth and transit-oriented development. In Mineola, for example, an intermodal transit center was built adjacent to the LIRR station, to accommodate commuter parking as well as buses. One of the biggest developments is in Wyandanch in Suffolk County.

Known as Wyandanch Rising, the planning for this development began in about 2004. The ambitious project includes new housing, retail, streetscape improvements, and a new train station. New York State launched its Downtown Revitalization Initiative in 2016, selecting one village in each region of the state per round of grants. Long Island communities selected for these grants so far have included Westbury, Hicksville, Central Islip, Baldwin, Amityville, and Huntington Station. In 2024, a plan was approved to create a Melville Town Center in an area that had for decades been mainly office parks with large parking lots.

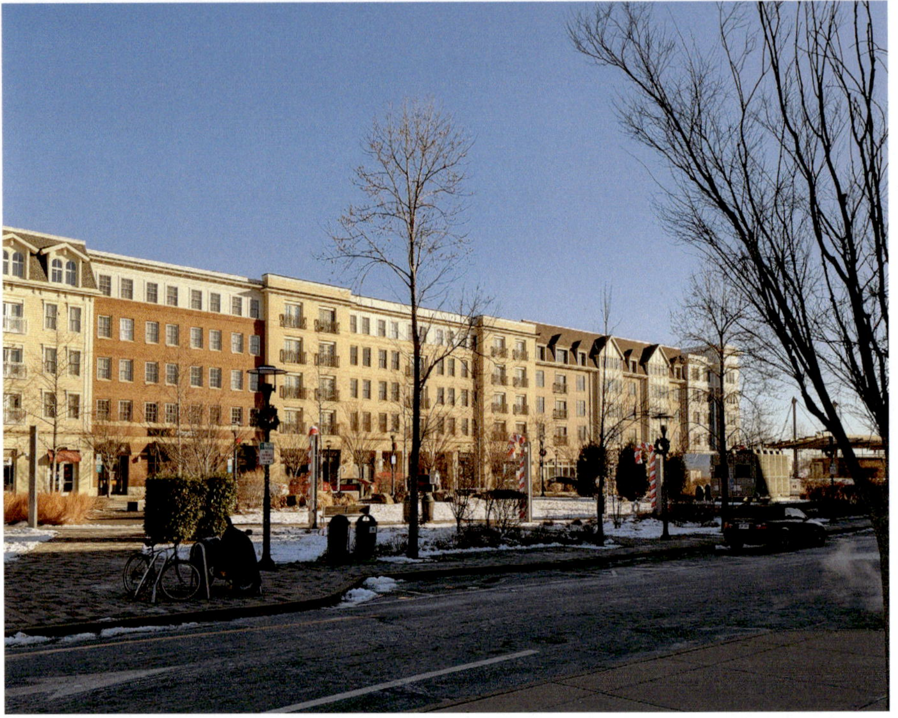

The Suffolk County community of Wyandanch has had major new development near the railroad station as part of an overall effort called Wyandanch Rising.

Opposite above: An office park area of Melville was approved in 2024 to be redeveloped to become a walkable downtown called Melville Town Center.

Opposite below: A successful Long Island downtown has a mix of retail, residential, and commercial and is walkable. Seen here is Babylon in Suffolk County.

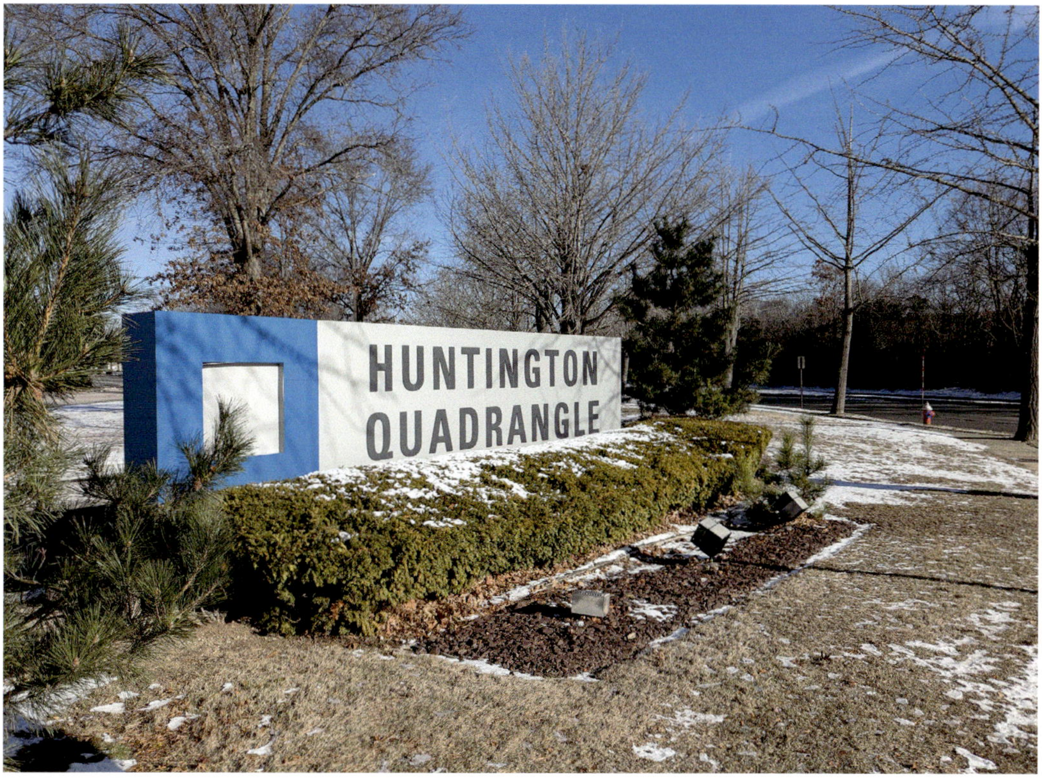

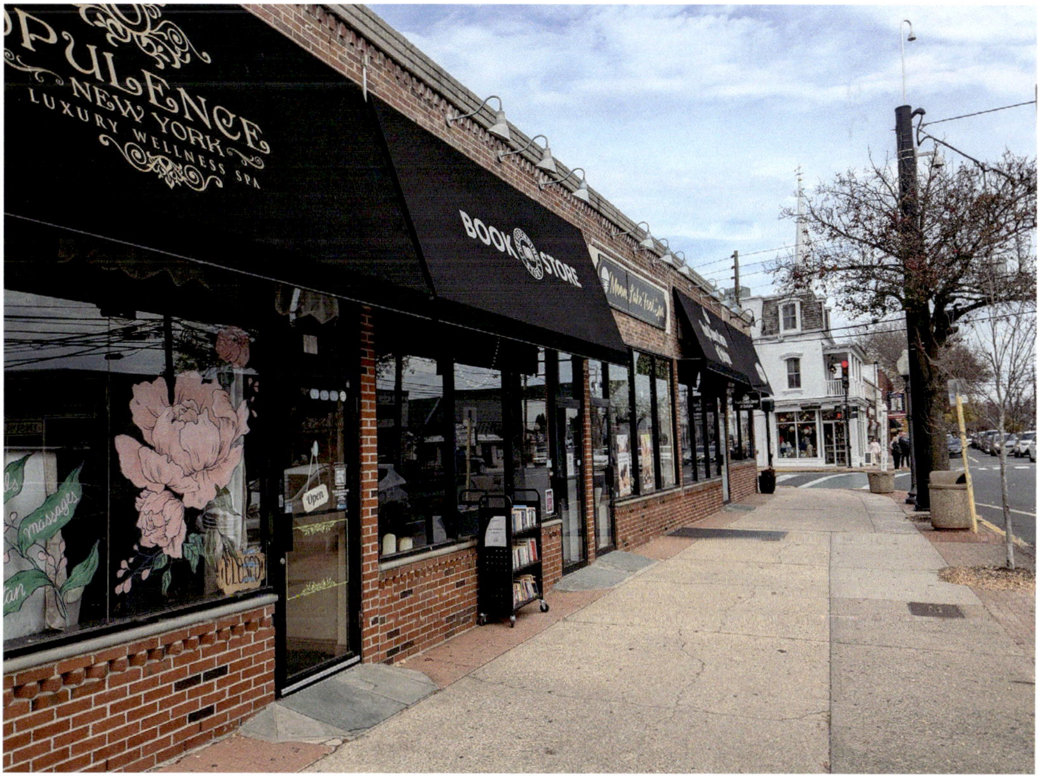

County Exec Indicted (2016)

There have been many comings and goings in Island politics since 2000, including indictments of several key politicians, shifts in power, and most recently the bizarre case of Congressman George Santos. On October 20, 2016, Nassau County Executive Edward Mangano (R—served two terms, from 2010 to 2017) was indicted on thirteen federal counts of fraud and bribery having to do with the fraudulent awarding of county contracts and loans to restauranteur Harendra Singh in exchange for favors such as a no-show $450,000 job for his wife, a massage chair, and five paid vacations. The incidents took place between January 2010 and February 2015, according to the evidence presented at trial. In May 2018, the Manganos' trial ended in a hung jury. After a seven-week retrial in early 2019, Mangano and his wife were both found guilty. On April 14, 2022, Ed Mangano was sentenced to twelve years in prison and ordered to pay a $20,000 fine, and his wife Linda was sentenced to fifteen months in prison for obstructing a grand jury by lying to the FBI in 2015; she was released in February 2023 after serving five months. Town of Oyster Bay Supervisor John Venditto (R) was also indicted in 2016 for his part in the scheme (helping Singh secure Town of Oyster bay-backed loans totaling about $20 million), but was acquitted. He was later found guilty of state corruption charges but did not serve any time.

PRESS RELEASE

Former Nassau County Executive Edward Mangano and His Wife Linda Mangano Sentenced for Corruption and Related Charges

Thursday, April 14, 2022

For Immediate Release

U.S. Attorney's Office, Eastern District of New York

Earlier today, at the federal courthouse in Central Islip, Edward Mangano, the former Nassau County Executive, and his wife Linda Mangano were sentenced by United States District Judge Joan M. Azrack to 12 years, and 15 months', imprisonment, respectively, following their convictions after a seven-week trial. Edward Mangano was convicted of multiple counts of accepting bribes and kickbacks in exchange for official government action, and for conspiracy to obstruct justice. Linda Mangano was also convicted of conspiracy to obstruct justice, obstruction of justice and making false statements to Federal Bureau of Investigation (FBI) agents in connection with her employment by Long Island restaurateur Harendra Singh. Edward Mangano was also ordered to pay a $20,000 fine.

A 2022 federal government press release announced the sentencing of former Nassau County Executive Ed Mangano and his wife Linda.

Trump Rallies on Long Island (2016, 2024)

On April 6, 2016, presidential candidate Donald Trump held a rally at the Grumman facility in Bethpage. Eight days later, he appeared as the headliner at a fundraiser in Patchogue. By this time, he was not yet the presumptive nominee, but the events were well attended. Eight years later during his third presidential campaign, he held a rally at the Nassau Coliseum on September 18, 2024. The rally was scheduled for the day that Trump was originally due to be sentenced in his hush money felony trial and had to be in New York anyway; the sentencing date was postponed by the judge, but the rally went on as planned. The parking lot opened at 9 a.m., gates to get inside the Coliseum opened at 3 p.m., the first speeches began a couple of hours later, and Trump appeared just after 7 p.m. At the time, much of the media questioned Trump's reasoning for appearing in a clearly non-battleground state (it was his second New York rally; in May, he held one at Crotona Park in the Bronx). During his speech, Trump told the crowd that he was going to win New York State and made promises to turn around what he called a failing state. Though he did not win the state, he did significantly better in New York than the previous two elections—getting 44.2 percent of the vote; in 2020, he only had 37.7 percent of the state's vote and in 2016 36.8 percent.

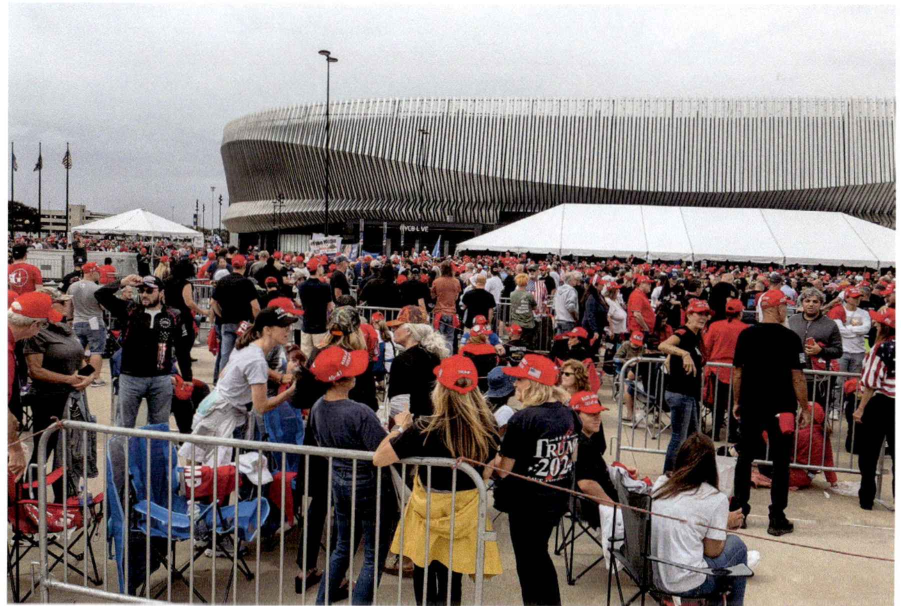

A crowd of people waits to get into Nassau Coliseum for Donald Trump's rally on September 18, 2024. He had previously held a rally on Long Island in 2016 when he appeared in Bethpage.

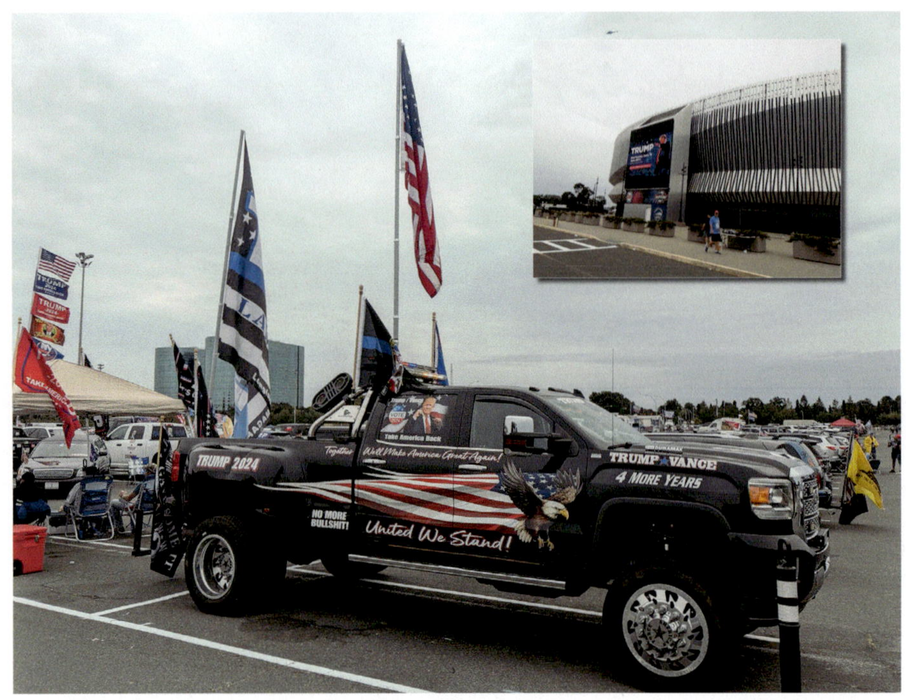

A customized pickup truck at the Trump rally at Nassau Coliseum, 2024. Inset: The front of Nassau Coliseum advertised his appearance there on September 18, 2024.

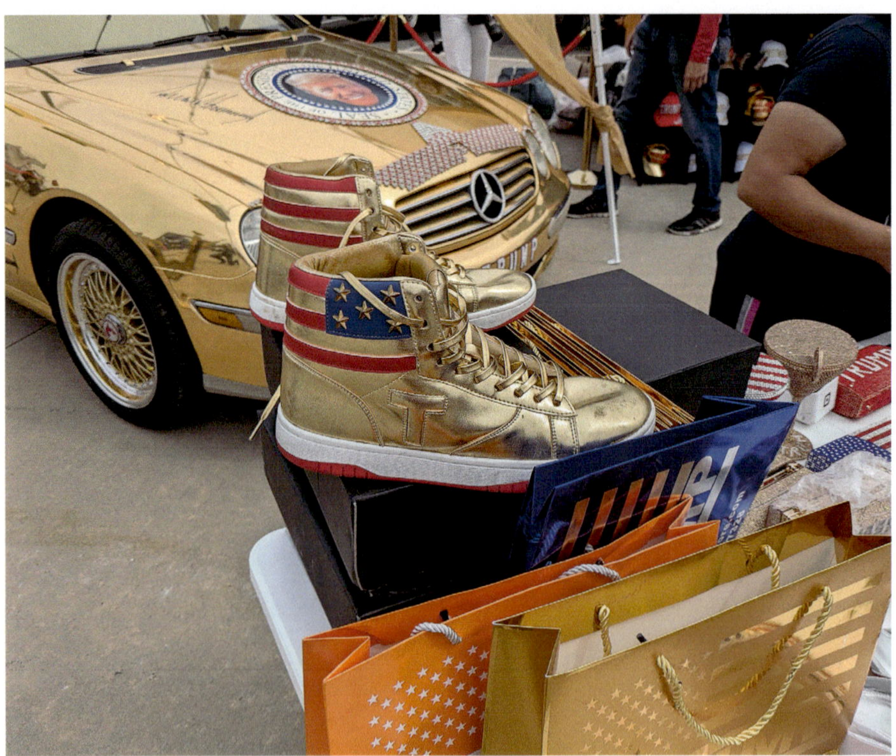

A pair of the Trump gold sneakers on display next to a golden Trump car at his rally.

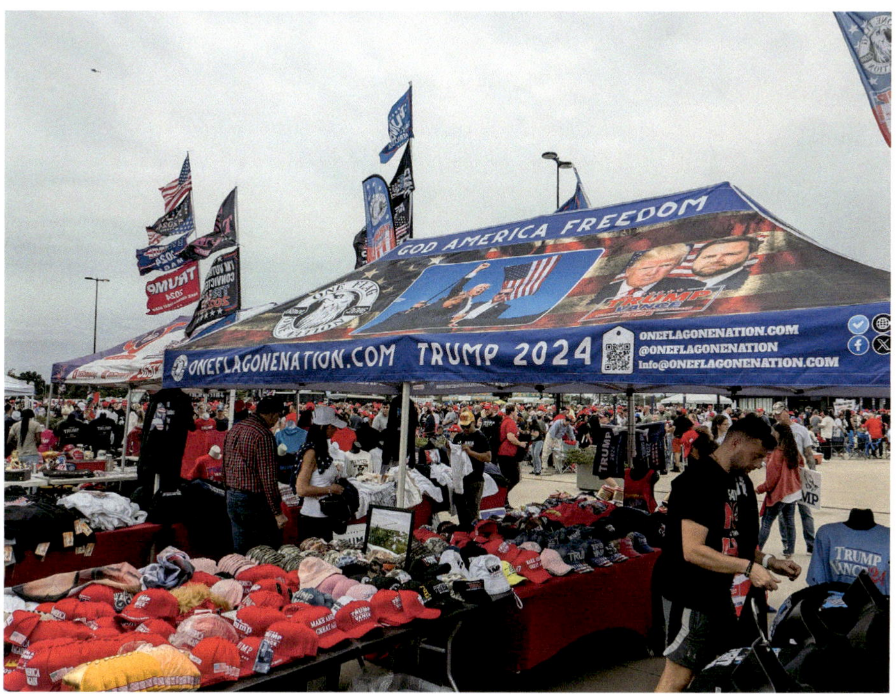

One of the many merchandise stands set up outside Nassau Coliseum in advance of Trump's rally there.

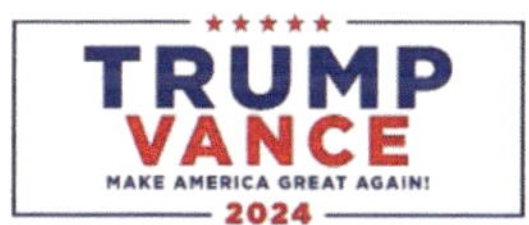

GUEST INSTRUCTIONS

We look forward to welcoming you to **President Donald J. Trump's Rally in Uniondale, New York on Wednesday, September 18th, 2024.** Please carefully review the following details and instructions to ensure smooth entry into the event.

Venue Information
Nassau Veterans Memorial Coliseum
1255 Hempstead Tpke.
Uniondale, NY 11553

This event will be **INDOORS.**

Guest Arrival Information
The line will begin to form early. Parking will open at 9:00 AM. Doors open at 3:00 PM. Event pre-programming will begin promptly at 4:30 PM. President Donald J. Trump's remarks will begin at 7.00 PM. **Please arrive no later than 4:00 PM**

Food and beverage will be available for purchase within the venue.

Parking Information
Parking will be available at 1255 Hempstead Tpke. ADA parking is limited at the venue and will be strictly reserved for individuals with an ADA parking placard.

Guests should access parking from Hempstead TPKE as illustrated in the image below.

The official instructions to attendees of the Uniondale Trump rally were sent to everyone who registered.

Legalized Weed (2016)

After being considered an illegal substance in New York for almost ninety years, medical cannabis finally became legal in 2016, and then in 2021, recreational cannabis was legalized in New York State. What followed on Long Island was the opening of the first marijuana dispensaries. As of 2025, there were five New York State Registered Medical cannabis dispensaries on Long Island; two in Nassau County (Carle Place and Long Beach) and three in Suffolk (Riverhead, Farmingdale, and Huntington Station). Though selling recreational weed is now legal with the proper licensing, Long Island towns have their individual zoning restrictions that dictate where dispensaries can open. The Town of Babylon, for example, requires that dispensaries must be in an industrial area, and have to be 1,000 feet away from residential areas, 200 feet away from religious properties, 500 feet away from schools, libraries, education facilities, parks, playgrounds, dance studios, gymnasiums, or any places where youth congregate. Due to those limitations, East Farmingdale wound up being an ideal spot; by 2024, there were three dispensaries there.

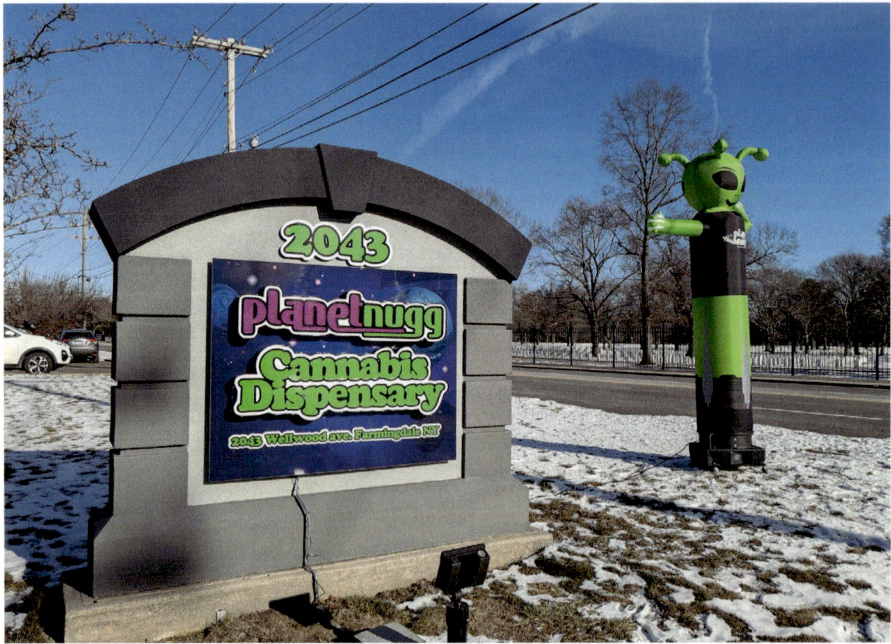

A weed dispensary in East Farmingdale.

Long Island Turns Red (2016)

Through the course of the first quarter of the twenty-first century, Long Island has changed back and forth from leaning blue to leaning red, but as of 2016, it began trending red. From 2004 to 2023, Suffolk County was run by Democratic county executives—first Steve Levy and then Steve Bellone. In the 2023 election, Bellone would not run again because of term limits. Republican Ed Romaine was elected over Democrat Dave Calone. In Nassau County, party control went back and forth over the first quarter of the twenty-first century, with Democrat Tom Suozzi holding the office from 2002 to 2009, then handing it over to Republican Ed Mangano from 2010 to 2017. Democrat Laura Curran was elected in 2017 and was county executive until 2021; she was defeated in her reelection bid by Republican Bruce Blakeman. Though there were a few blue surprises in the 2024 election—including Laura Gillen's victory over Republican incumbent Anthony D'Esposito in New York's 2nd Congressional District—2024 was the first time since 1988 that the Republican presidential candidate won Nassau County since 1988 (Trump got nearly 51 percent of the Nassau vote in 2024). Suffolk County had voted blue in every presidential election from 1996 to 2012, but turned red in 2016, 2020, and 2024.

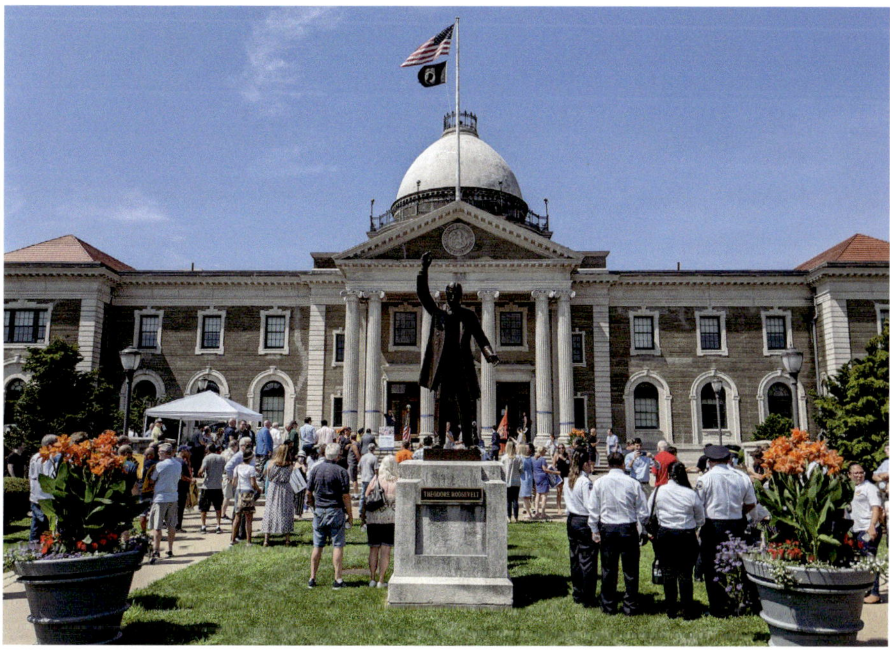

A rally for incumbent Nassau County Executive Laura Curran (D) in Mineola, August 18, 2021. She lost the election to Bruce Blakeman (R).

Filming *The Irishman* (2017)

Key scenes from the epic 2019 Martin Scorsese movie *The Irishman* were filmed in September 2017 in Willison Park. The authentically vintage interior of local landmark Hildebrandt's Restaurant (vintage 1920s) was used for a scene featuring Al Pacino and Robert DeNiro, which took place on November 22, 1963, as news of the Kennedy assassination played on the television in the restaurant. About seventy cast and crew were on set during the filming, including director Martin Scorsese. Meanwhile, the interior of the now-defunct Mineola diner Biscuits and Barbecue was prepped, and filming took place inside, but the scene did not make it to the movie. Other Long Island filming locations included Baldwin and Shirley. The Irishman received ten Oscar nominations at the 92nd Academy Awards, including Best Picture, Best Director, and Best Supporting Actor, though it did not win any. That film was just one of many movies and television shows that were shot on the island in the first quarter of the twenty-first century, including HBO's *The Affair* (Montauk, 2014–2019), USA's *Royal Pains* (various locations, 2009–2016), and *The Wolf of Wall Street* (Hamptons, 2013).

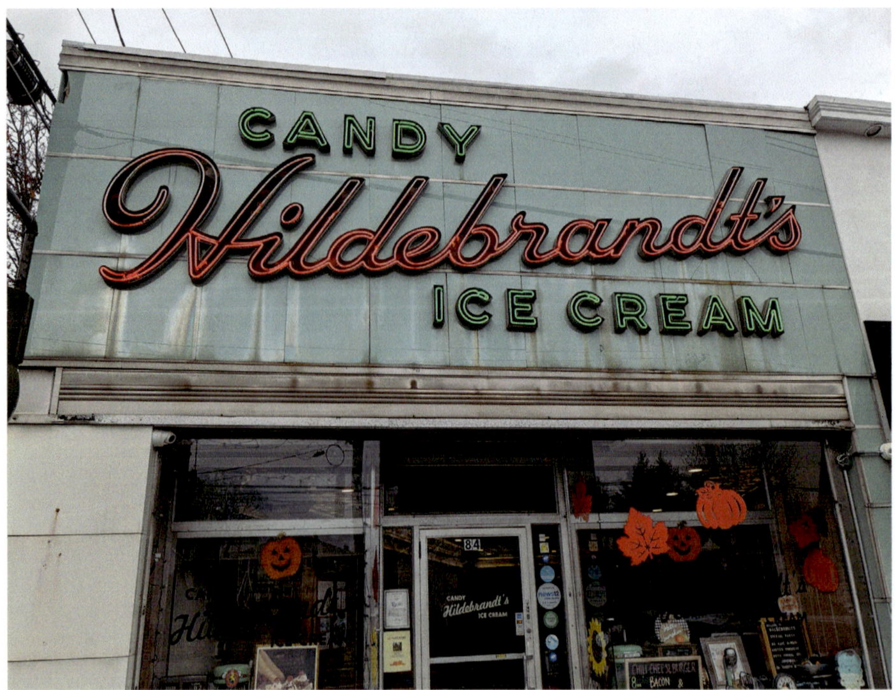

Hildebrandt's restaurant in Williston Park was used to shoot a key scene in the 2017 movie *The Irishman.*

The First Casino (2017)

In 2013, New York State's constitution was amended to allow for the existence of commercial casinos (there had been Native American-owned casinos in the state since 1993). At first, they mostly opened in upstate New York. Long Island finally got a casino a few years later when Jake's 58 Casino Hotel opened in May 2017 at exit 58 off the LIE (Islandia) offering off track betting as well as slot machines in what was formerly a Marriott hotel. The casino, Long Island's first and one of only two government-owned casinos in the United States, features 100 electronic table games and 1,000 video and electronic slot machines. The hotel portion offers 200 rooms. In 2024, a $210 million expansion was announced that would double the number of terminals to 2,000 by 2026 and add a parking garage to more than triple the number of parking spaces, a convention center, and an outdoor terrace. Profits, for the most part, go to the New York State Education Department and to the host county, Suffolk County. Islandia village property taxes were projected to be eliminated because of the casino's contributions to the local tax base. As of November 2024, total payouts (winnings) from the casino were $836,558,707.

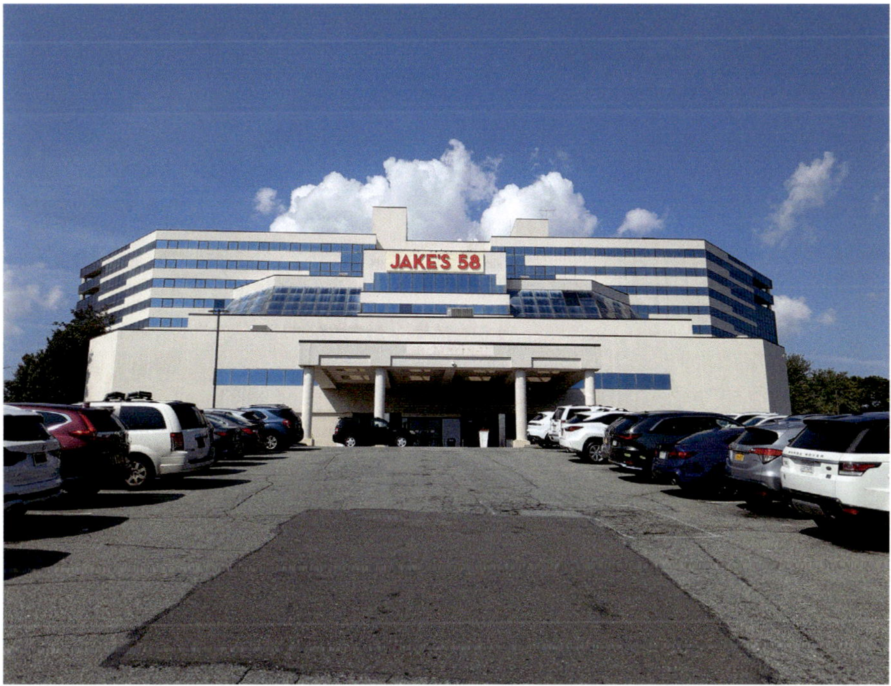

Jake's 58 Casino in Islandia is just off the Long Island Expressway.

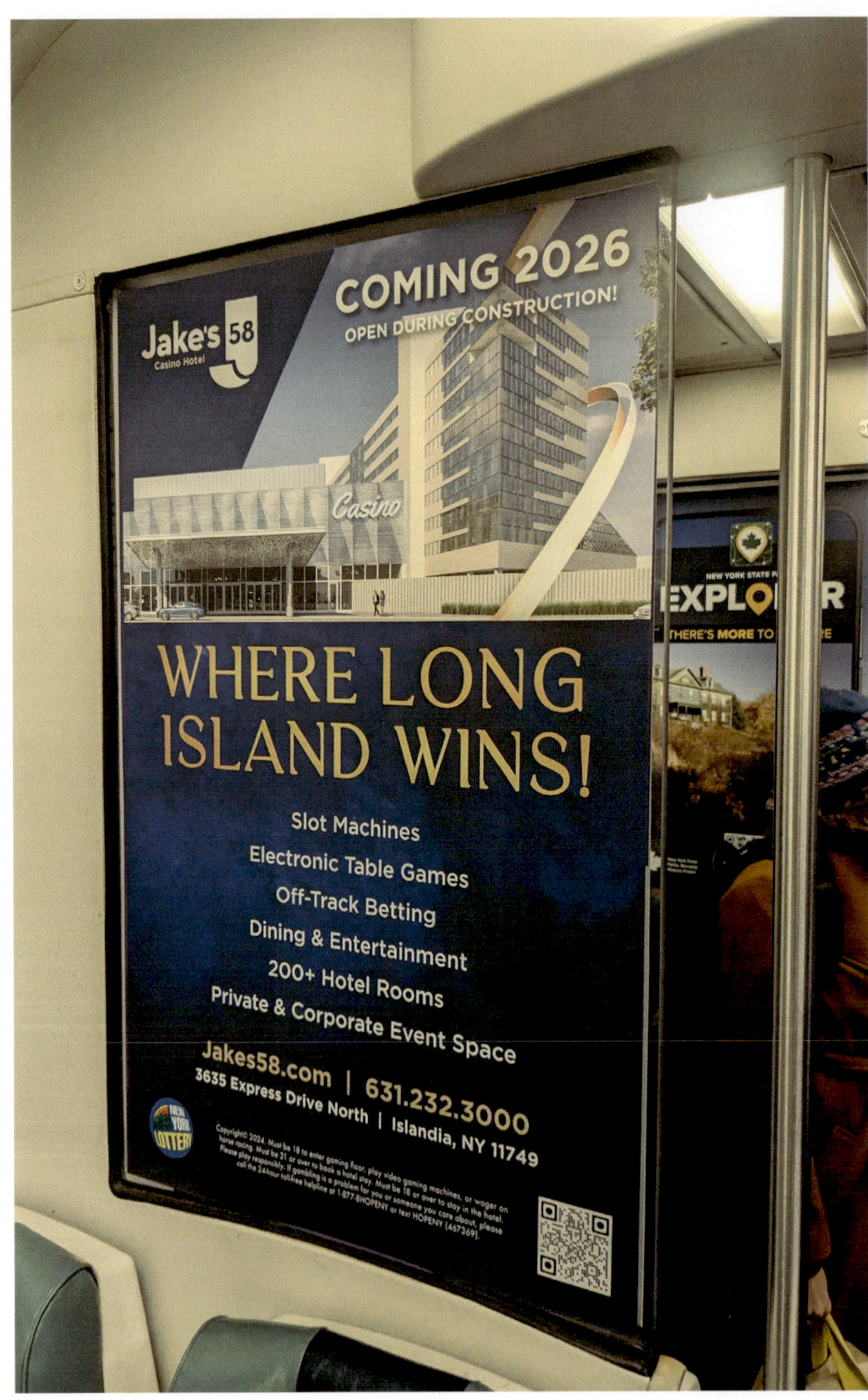

An advertisement in an LIRR train car promoting the upcoming expansion of the Jake's 58 Casino.

Restoring the Grist Mill (2018)

The old Robeson-Williams grist mill in downtown Roslyn Village has been a fixture since it was built in the early eighteenth century; it is considered one of the island's oldest remaining historic treasures. In 1790, the grist mill's owner was visited by President George Washington at his nearby home. After serving as a mill for a century and a half, it was converted into a tearoom in 1920 (the Roslyn Mill Tea House) and served in that capacity until 1974. After that point, however, it was subject to decay and weathering that threatened its very existence. It remained shuttered during the years after its teahouse days. After numerous failed attempts, restoration was finally begun in earnest in 2018 after several grants had been received. In 2020, the mill was lifted 8 feet off its foundation and a new one poured before the mill was lowered again. On May 28, 2022, the structure was lowered to street level for the first time in a century. In December 2023, the Roslyn Landmark Society received a $500,000 grant from the Save America's Treasures program, through the National Park Service.

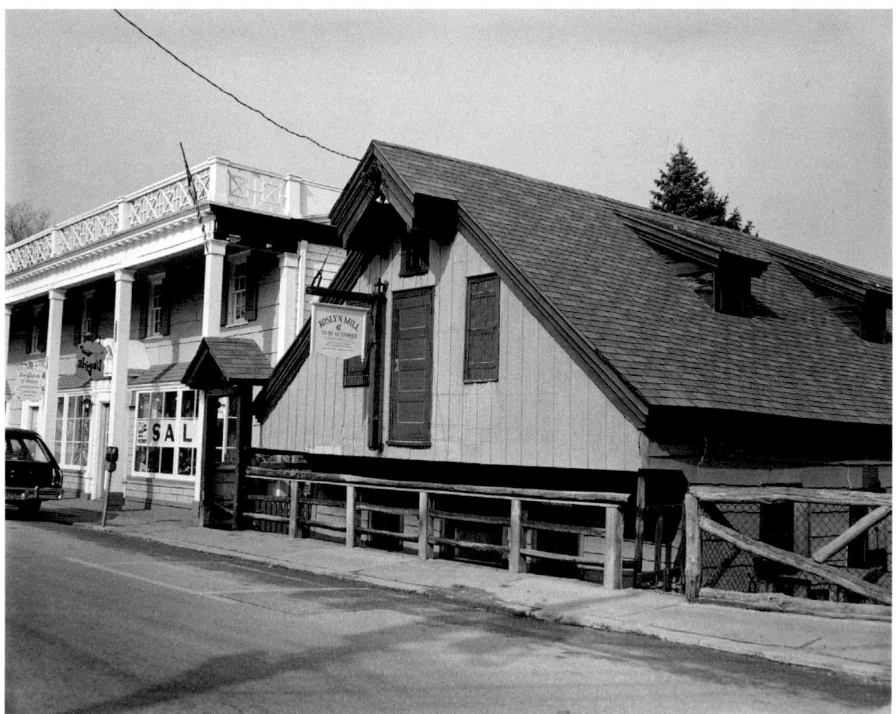

The historic eighteenth-century Roslyn Grist Mill in the 1970s, just after it was a teahouse, awaiting restoration.

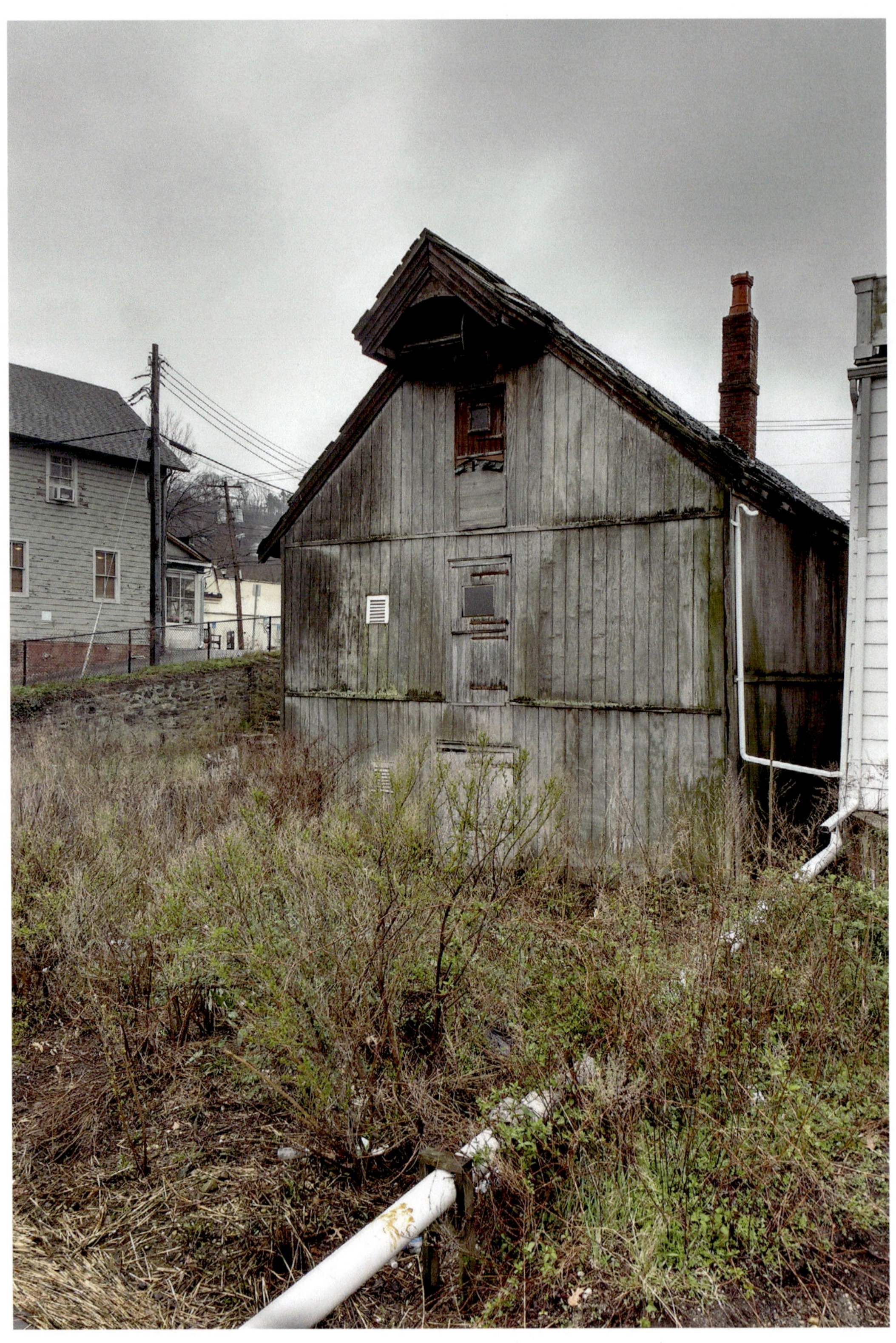

The grist mill, seen here in 2016, deteriorated over the years and was still awaiting restoration.

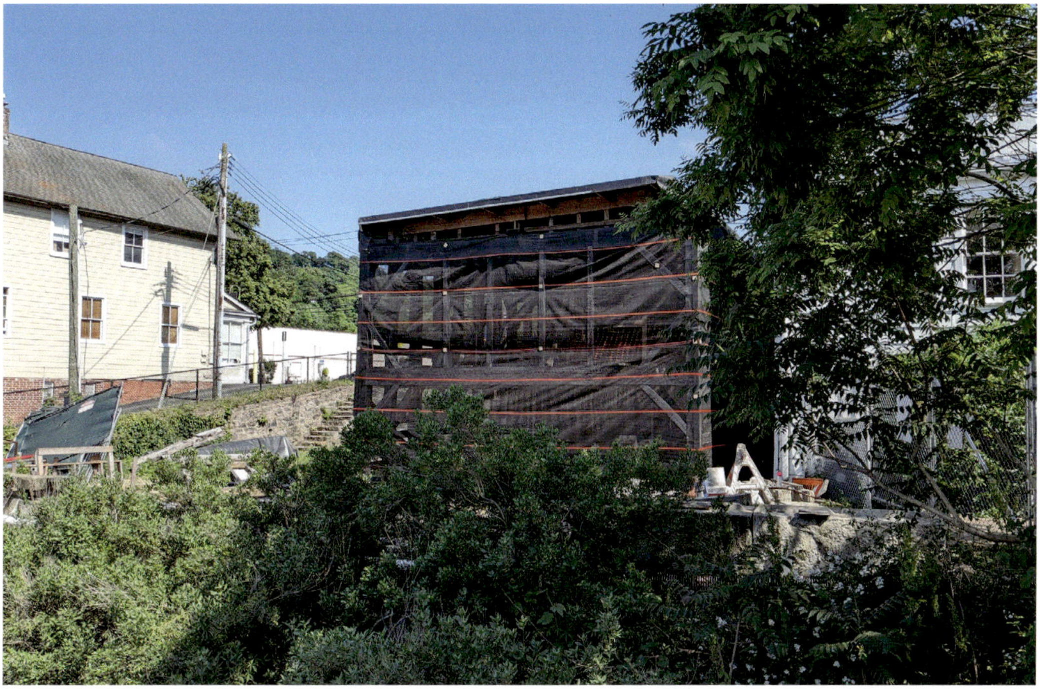

The back of the grist mill in May 2024 as it was finally being reconstructed.

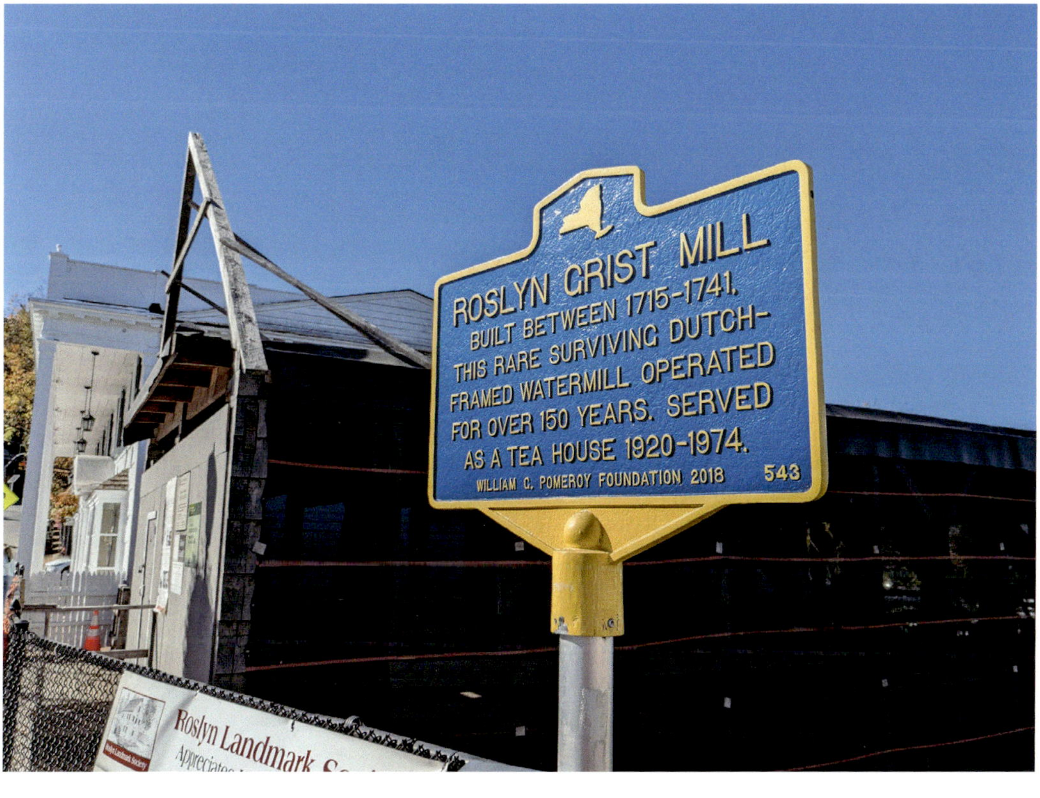

A 2018 historical marker next to the grist mill, seen here in November 2024 while being restored.

At Grade Crossing Elimination (2019)

When William K. Vanderbilt II built his Long Island Motor Parkway (aka Vanderbilt Motor Parkway) starting in 1908, one of its amazing features was that it included no at-grade crossings. All features were either crossed over or under—there were sixty-five bridges along the parkway. The LIRR, tracing its Long Island roots back to the 1840s, did not have that beneficial feature. In fact, the world's first train-automobile collision happened in 1901 on Post Avenue just west of Westbury Station. Several years later, the Post Avenue at-grade crossing was converted to a bridge carrying the railroad. Grade crossing safety has been an issue for many years; there were six fatal crashes at grade crossing locations in the LIRR Main Line corridor from 2007 to 2017, prompting the grade crossing elimination program. In recent years, several key at-grade crossings have been eliminated as part of the LIRR Expansion Project from Floral Park to Hicksville, including Covert Avenue in New Hyde Park, Willis Avenue in Mineola, and School Street in Westbury. The last was done not long after a fatal accident at the crossing in 2019, when three people were killed when a train struck their car on the tracks. The grade crossings were eliminated by taking the roadways under the tracks via bridge structures to support the rail service.

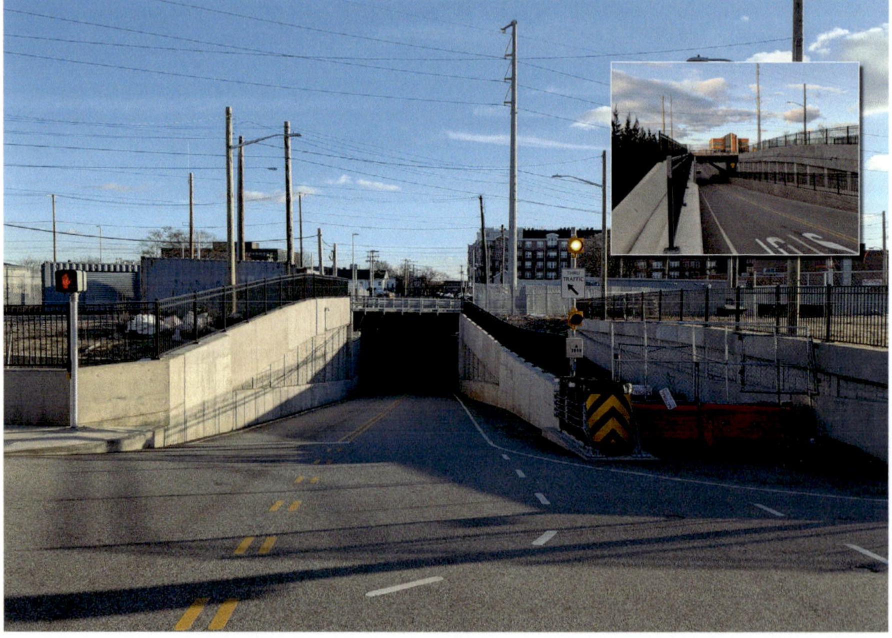

At-grade crossing elimination took place in several locations along the main branch of the LIRR, including Willis Avenue and 2nd Street in Mineola and School Street in Westbury (inset).

Plum Island Sale Prevented (2020)

This 840-acre island off the eastern tip of Orient Point was home to a military installment called Fort Terry (built in 1897) that was deactivated after World War II. In 1952, the Army Chemical Corps took over the facilities and in 1954, it went to the U.S. Department of Agriculture, and it housed the Plum Island Animal Disease Center (PIADC), which included laboratories and livestock holding pens for research purposes. In 2005, the PIADC was scheduled to close and relocate to Kansas, and in 2008, Congress approved legislation requiring that Plum Island be sold to help fund the new DHS National Bio and Agro-Defense Facility in Manhattan, Kansas. In 2013, the government announced plans to sell Plum Island, but in December 2020, Congress passed the Omnibus Budget bill that saved Plum Island from the auction block, restoring the normal disposal procedure for federal property instead of auctioning it to the highest bidder. The island is home to more than 500 plant and animal species, 111 of which are species of special concern. The island's wildlife include 200 species of birds, over 200 species of moths, nine types of mammals, and five kinds of reptiles.

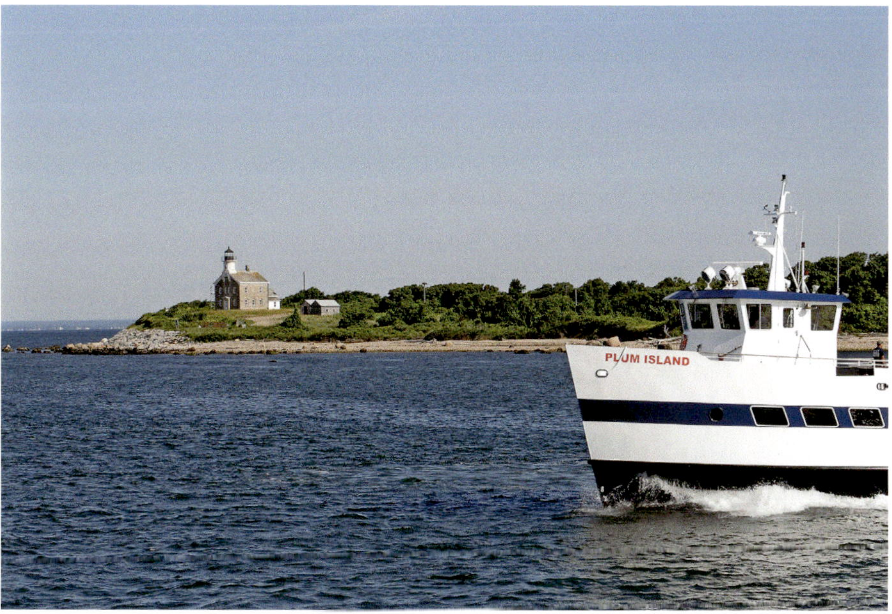

A 2007 Department of Agriculture photo shows the MS Plum Island making the crossing between Orient Point and Plum Island. It made the crossing several times a day, carrying passengers and cargo as part of normal Plum Island Animal Disease Center operations.

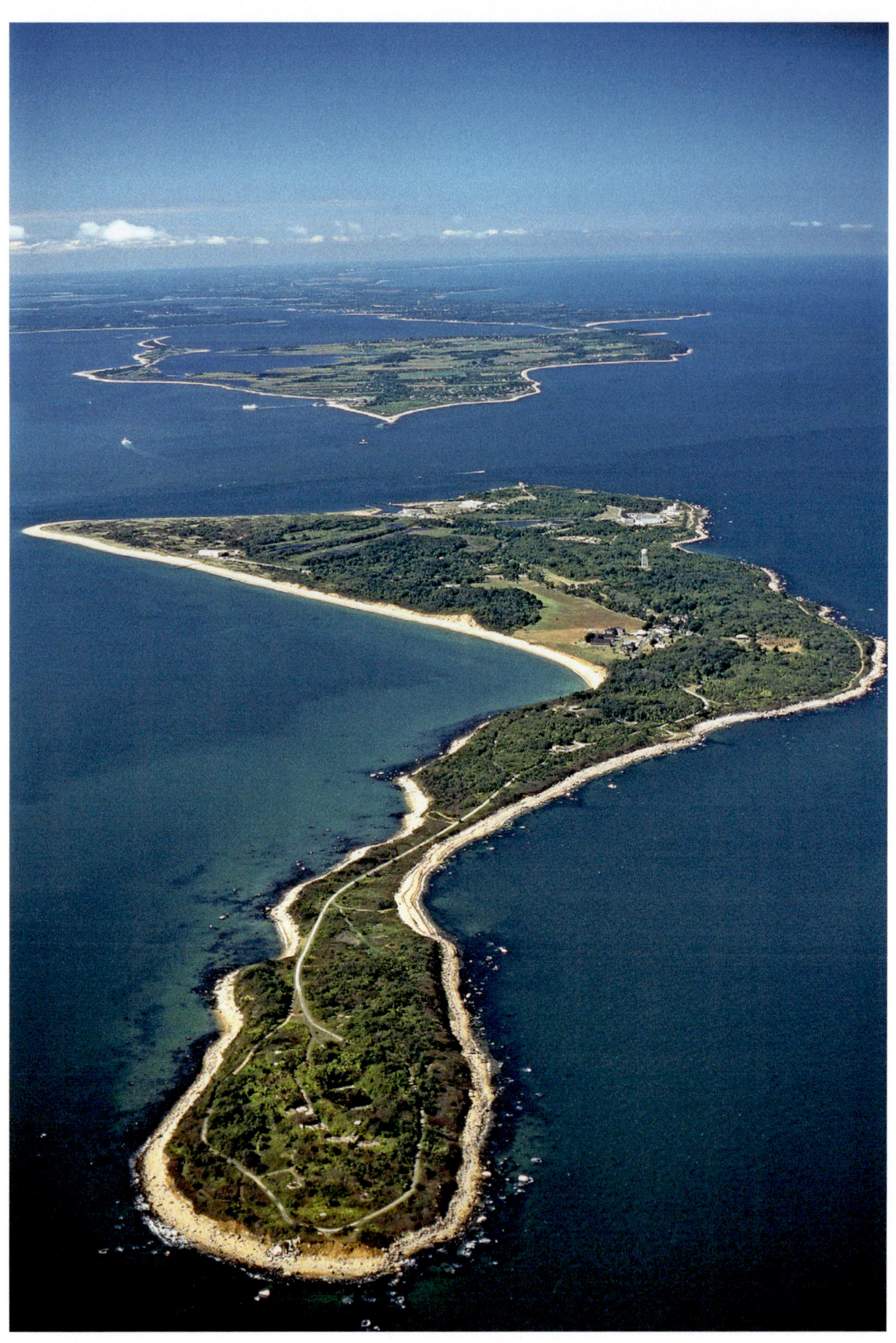

A 2011 aerial view of Plum Island.

Tales from a Pandemic (2020)

We had all started hearing about a dangerous new virus called COVID-19 by January 2020, and we were hopeful it would not spread in this country. When the first confirmed case of COVID-19 in New York City was announced on March 1, 2020, and then the first case in Nassau County was announced on March 5, low-key panic began to set in. I remember being in the Mattituck library bathroom on March 8 and feeling anxious at the newly posted signs stressing the importance of hand washing and not touching things. On March 12, Governor Andrew Cuomo banned gatherings of more than 500 people (aka no more concerts), and on March 16, gatherings were limited to fifty people. As cases continued to increase, New York State went on "Pause" on March 22, with all non-essential businesses ordered shut. The first couple of months most of us stayed home except to try to stockpile essentials such as toilet paper. We were told the state would begin to reopen when the COVID case numbers stabilized. The "Phase 1" reopening of Long Island happened on May 27, but it only meant that curbside retail pickup could occur, and construction and manufacturing could resume. Mask wearing and social distancing helped Long Island meet the metrics for the next step, and we were cleared to proceed to "Phase 2" of the reopening on June 10. Restaurants would be able to offer outdoor seating, and stores could reopen with masks required and everyone keeping 6 feet apart on lines. Non-essential workers could also return to their offices. June 24 was the first day of "Phase 3" of the reopening on Long Island, when restaurants could finally have indoor dining once again—albeit at a 50 percent capacity. On July 9, museums were allowed to reopen, and on July 10, malls were finally allowed to reopen. The pre-vaccine months that followed were a strange and fearful time—we were trying to do normal activities but also stay away from people. COVID testing during this time had to be done at a clinic and often took days to get results back; it was not until November 2020 that the FDA approved rapid home COVID tests.

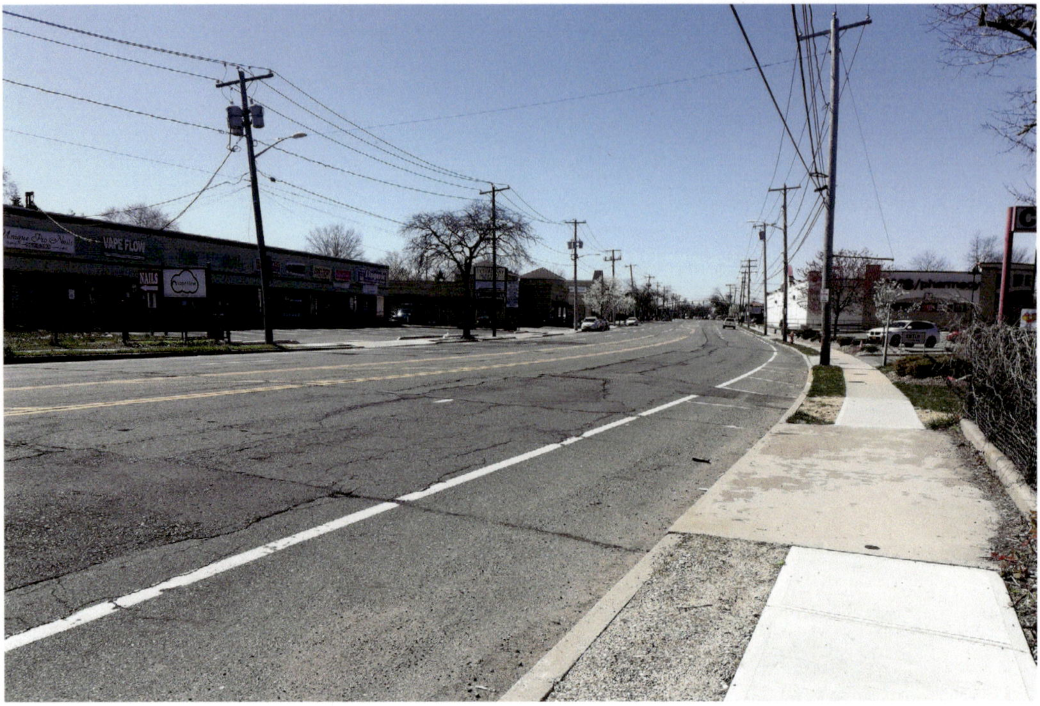

An empty Merrick Road in Merrick on April 6, 2020. During the early days of the pandemic, Long Islanders stayed home as much as possible.

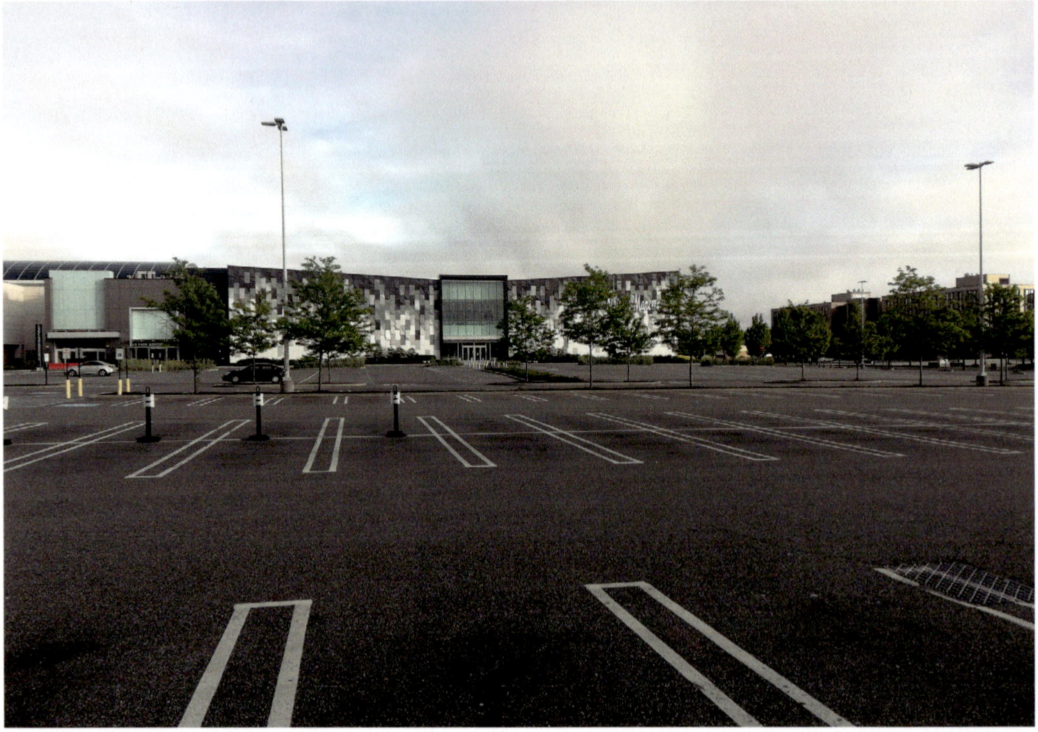

The Roosevelt Field Mall parking lot, May 27, 2020.

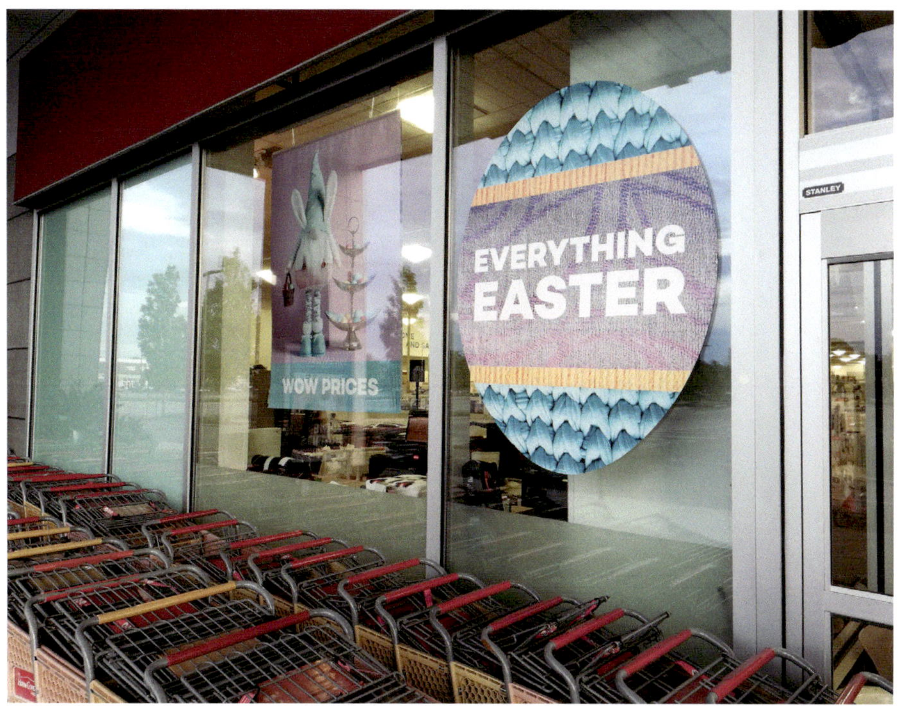

A sign for Easter merchandise remains in a craft store window on June 3, 2020. For months, retail displays were frozen in time at the moment the world shut down.

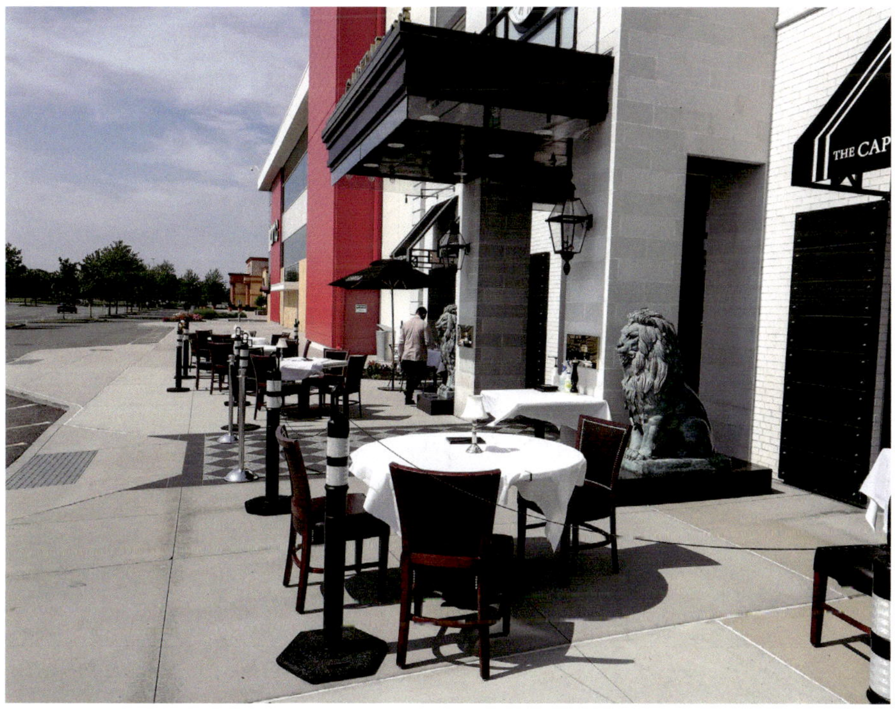

Tables set up at the Capital Grill in Garden City on the first day outdoor dining was allowed, June 10, 2020.

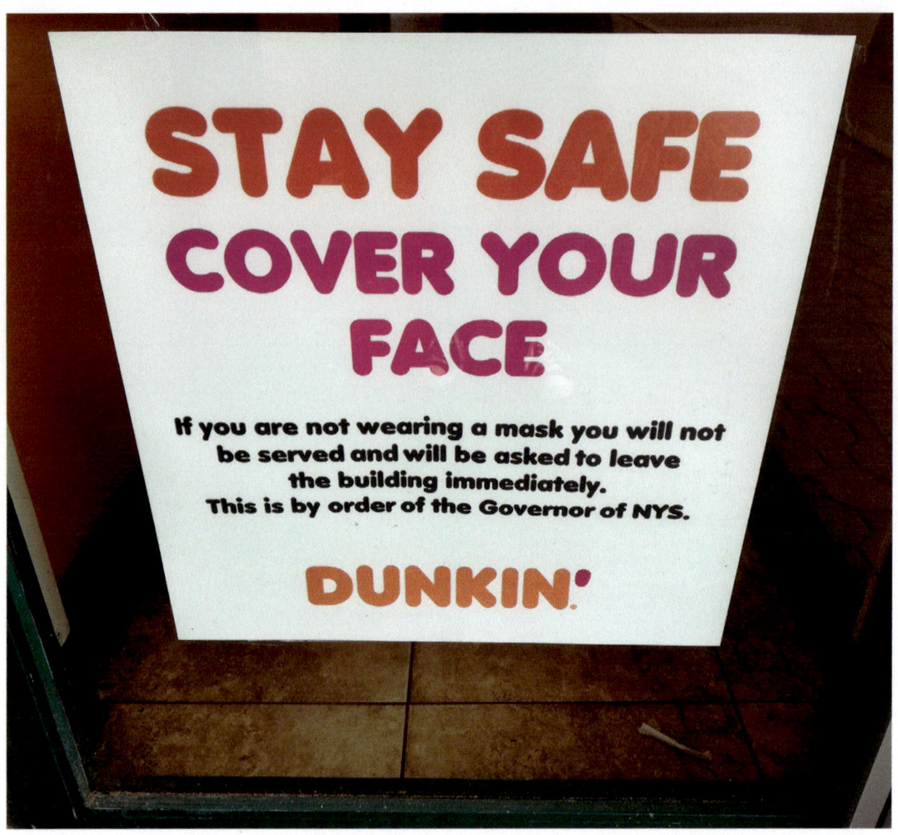

A sign on a Dunkin' Donuts door, June 12, 2020.

George Floyd Protests (2020)

The COVID pandemic was not the only reason the country was in turmoil in the spring of 2020. On May 25, a black man named George Floyd was killed by the violent actions of a white police officer in Minneapolis, Minnesota, after Floyd had been arrested. As news coverage and subsequent outrage over his death spread across the country, protests against racism and police brutality sprang up everywhere. There were at least forty-two documented protests at different locations throughout Long Island in the weeks that followed. The numbers of protesters at these events ranged from about a hundred to several thousand. These protests were mostly peaceful and resulted in only a few arrests; there was some property damage. Some local store owners boarded up their windows and doors to prevent damage and looting (during a time when the stores were closed already due to the pandemic shutdown), including at the Roosevelt Field mall.

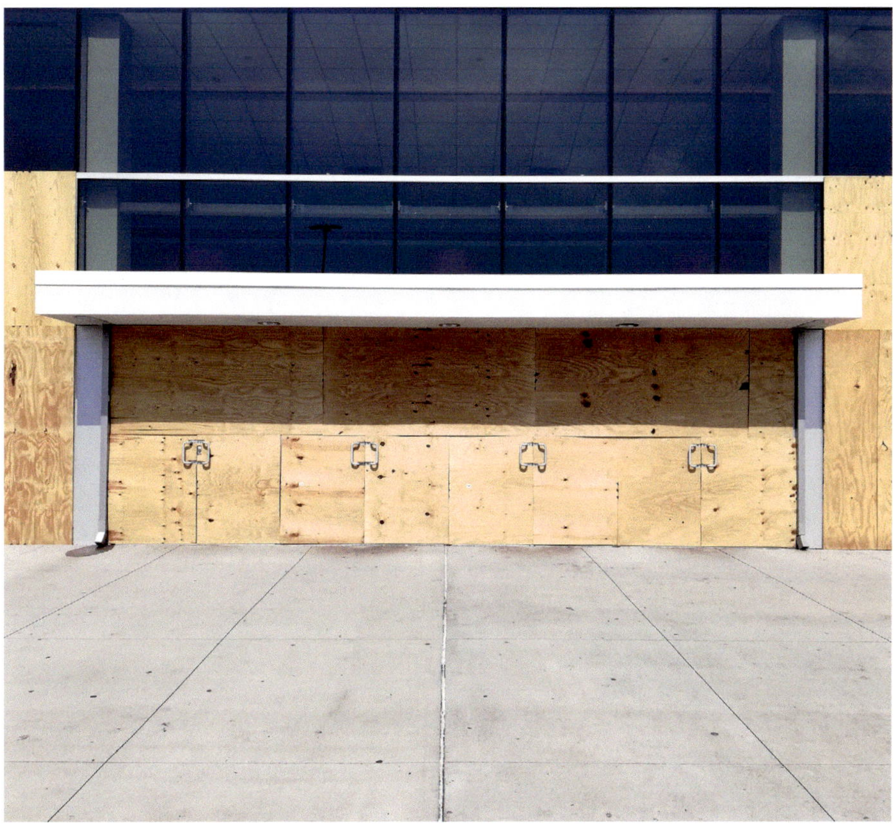

The AMC movie theater boarded up as a precaution during the George Floyd protests, June 2020.

Life After Vaccination (2021)

As the epidemic raged, major drug companies hurried to create an effective vaccine. In late 2020, the FDA gave emergency use authorization to two mRNA COVID-19 vaccines, the Pfizer-BioNTech and the Moderna. Vaccinations in the United States began to be administered on December 14, 2020, and became widely available in January 2021. Those initial vaccinations were a massive coordination effort and many were held at large-scale facilities such as the SUNY Old Westbury campus. The first booster shots became available in September 2021. With new variants and waning of the original doses' effectiveness, the peak for infections on Long Island actually came on January 3, 2022, when 18,906 people tested positive for COVID. A second booster shot was approved by the FDA in March 2022. Numbers continued to decrease after the January peak, and life became more normal—but it was a new normal. Though the workforce returned to their offices, for many, hybrid

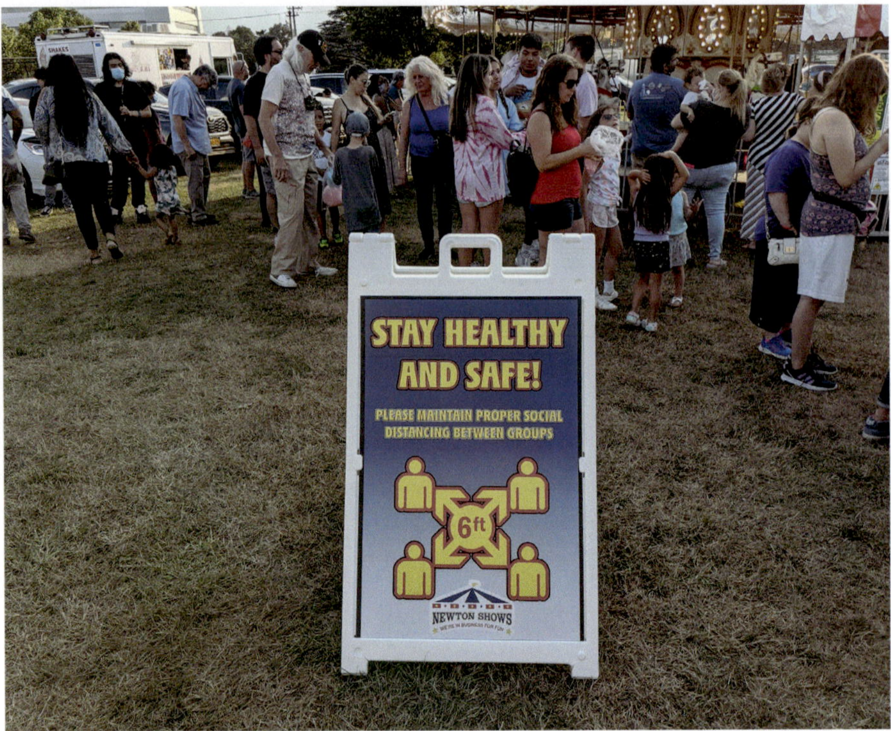

By July 2021, large gatherings were being allowed again. This carnival at Eisenhower Park was crowded with people who were clearly ready to go back to normal finally. Though the sign warned everyone to stay 6 feet apart, nobody listened.

work situations replaced five-day-a-week cubicle life, while other jobs became exclusively remote. The scheduled launch in 2020 of the new Glen Cove ferry service to Manhattan was postponed indefinitely due to COVID and the subsequent decline in commuters to the city. As of March 2024, 4,973 Nassau County residents and 5,837 Suffolk County residents had died from COVID. By the end of 2024, LIRR ridership had rebounded but still not quite returned to pre-COVID levels.

Moynihan Train Hall (2021)

For almost sixty years, Long Islanders taking the Long Island Rail Road into wondrous New York City emerged in the depressing, dingy low-ceilinged "new" Penn Station that replaced the magnificent McKim Mead & White Beaux Arts structure that was demolished in 1963. Once a bold visual statement, the station was now confined to underground and was replaced aboveground by Madison Square Garden and

One Penn Plaza. It was, to say the least, an uninspired entry point into one of the greatest cities in the world. In the 1990s, a plan was formulated that would extend Penn Station west, into a newly enclosed courtyard space of the old James Farley Post Office (1914, also McKim Mead & White) between Eighth and Ninth Avenues. The new complex (to which all Amtrak trains were relocated), designed by one of the most formidable modern architecture firms—Skidmore, Owings, & Merrill—was to be named after former senator Daniel Patrick Moynihan. It opened on January 1, 2021, in the midst of the COVID-19 pandemic, to mostly accolades. One of the complaints about the space is the lack of any seating at all within the main hall, leading to waiting travelers sitting on the floor or atop their bags. There is, however, a food court whose numerous eateries opened gradually over the next two years. Long Islanders riding into the city at the front of their trains (the Eighth Avenue end) wind up in the new hall, while those in the middle and back of the train still emerge in the old Penn Station (itself the subject of a makeover, see page 75).

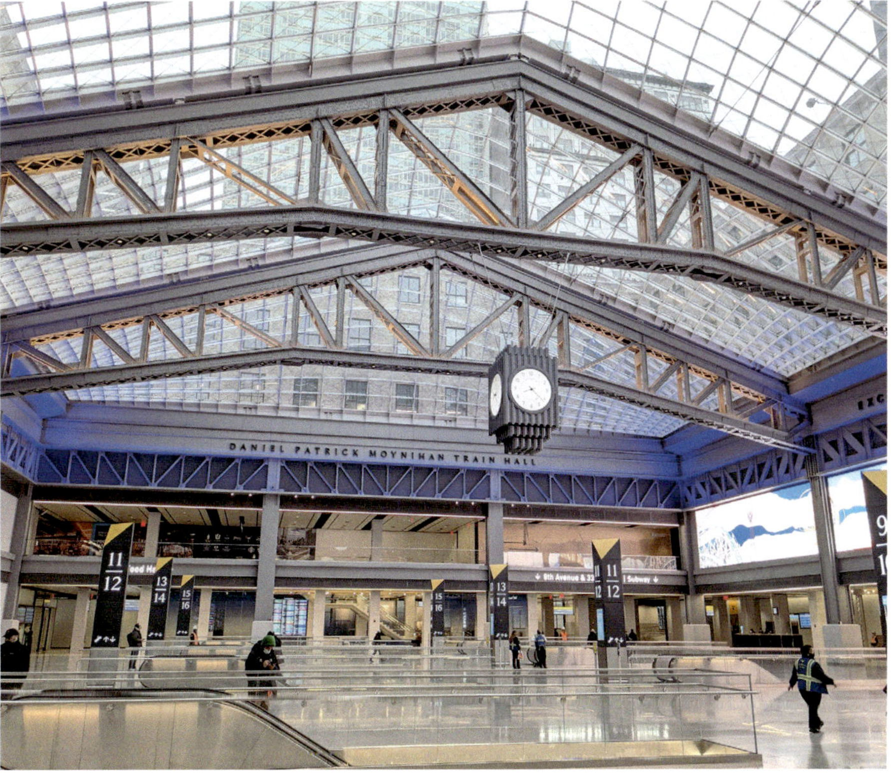

Moynihan Train Hall on January 4, 2021, just after it opened to the public. The new train hall serves the front end of arriving trains from Long Island, offering a visual treat to riders as compared to the more subdued old Penn Station.

UBS Arena Arrives (2021)

While the old Nassau Coliseum got a major facelift in 2017, its days as a major concert venue all but ended with the opening of the UBS Arena (built 2019–21; capacity 19,000) at the Belmont Park site in Elmont. One of the last big name acts at the Coliseum was Elton John in March 2022, and that was a rescheduled appearance from an earlier date. The new UBS venue was bigger, closer to New York City, and importantly, got its own LIRR station: Elmont UBS Arena (opened for full service in both directions October 2022). This allowed anyone to get there with relative ease from the city, without having to drive. And those who did choose to drive were offered shuttle bus service to take them from the expansive parking lots to the venue. The arena's website boasts that it has "more restrooms per person than any arena in Metro New York" and the "best sightlines in Metro New York." From the onset, the new venue attracted the biggest names in entertainment, including Genesis on their final tour, the Eagles, Roger Waters, and Billy Joel for New Year's Eve concerts. The storied NHL Islanders, after playing more than forty years based out of the Nassau Coliseum in Uniondale, moved to Brooklyn in 2015, then returned to the Coliseum for some games once it was renovated—but ultimately moved to the newly opened UBS Arena in Elmont in 2021.

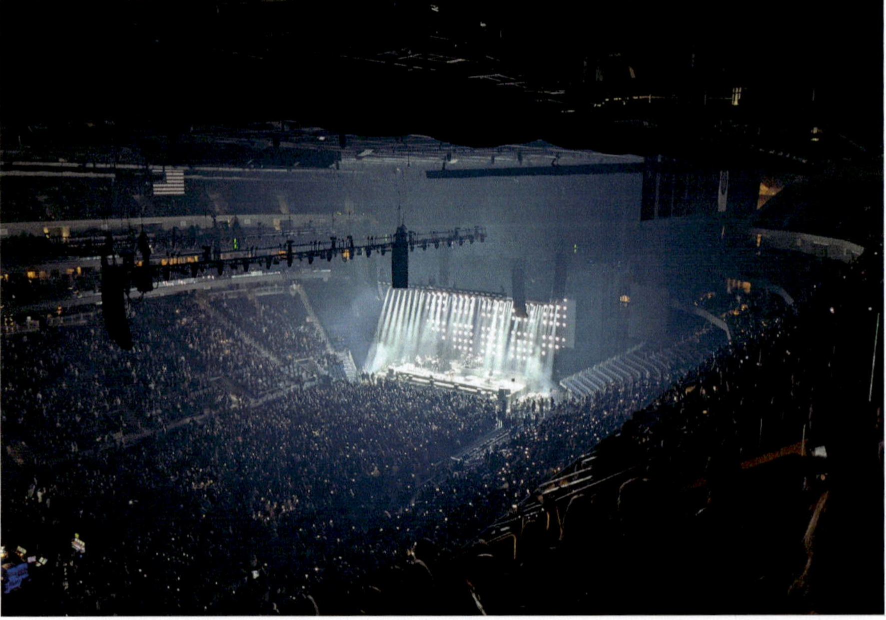

The rock band Genesis in concert at the UBS Arena, December 10, 2021, not long after it opened.

Pickleball Comes to Long Island (2021)

It is rare these days that a "new" sport takes the country by storm, but that is exactly what happened with pickleball, a cross between tennis, table tennis, and badminton with a touch of racquetball mixed in. Though the sport was first created in 1965 in Washington State, it took some years to catch on. The sport really took off in the Long Island region around 2021. As it grew in popularity, tennis courts began to be converted into smaller pickleball courts. As of 2024, county and town parks across the island had numerous pickleball courts—some permanent and some "portable" where nets could be set up and taken down on tennis courts. Pickleball leagues formed and tournaments were held. The sport was touted as perfect for all ages, including older persons with limited mobility. Jones Beach has ten pickleball courts, located directly behind the shuffleboard courts. The former longtime badminton courts on Merrick Avenue across from Eisenhower Park in Westbury were converted to thirteen pickleball courts in 2025. Because of the smaller court size and limited range of the ball, pickleball is an ideal indoor sport. It is especially popular as a doubles sport, with two players on each side of the net.

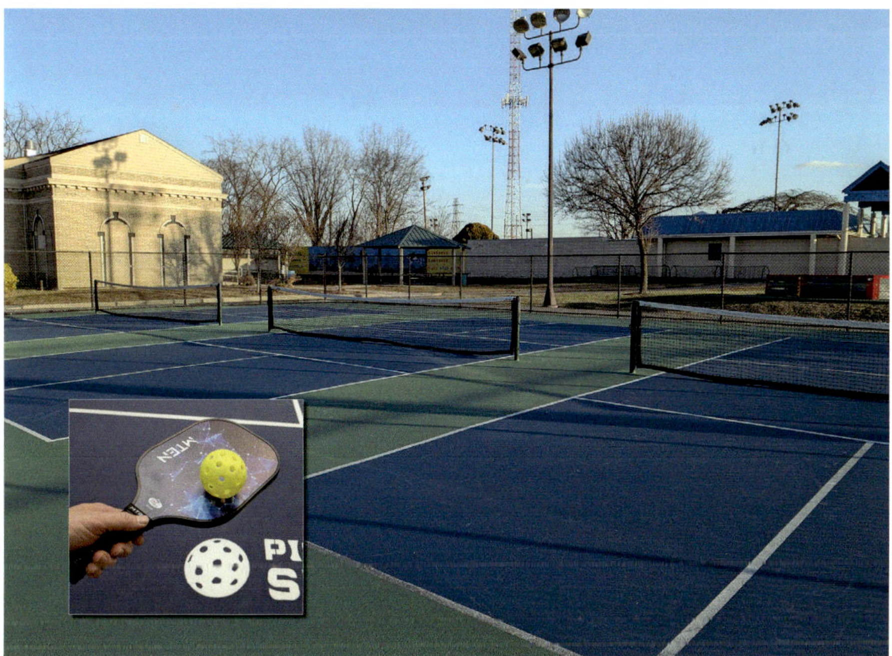

Pickleball is a huge hit on Long Island, with both indoor and outdoor courts opening at a rapid pace in the 2020s.

Third Track is Completed (2022)

The Third Track program was part of the massive $2.6 billion Long Island Rail Road Main Line Expansion Project. This ambitious project added a third track for 9.8 miles of the LIRR main line between Floral Park and Hicksville, to create expanded capacity for a projected increase in ridership. One of the most important benefits of this third track is the ability to go around disabled trains, instead of the traditional long delays of several trains waiting in line until the problem train was cleared up. The design-build contract was awarded in December 2017, and work was completed in October 2022, $100 million under budget. "This results in reduced train congestion and delays, true bi-directional service during peak hours, and a more reliable rail network. It will improve commutes and safety for over 300,000 daily riders LIRR system-wide. The project will make living and working on Long Island easier, ensuring the region's economic prosperity now and for the next century," according to the MTA website. In conjunction with Third Track work, several stations were completely reconstructed too, with crossover passages added at Carle Place and Westbury. A new parking structure was added at Westbury to hold over 600 vehicles. Eight at-grade rail crossings were eliminated under this program.

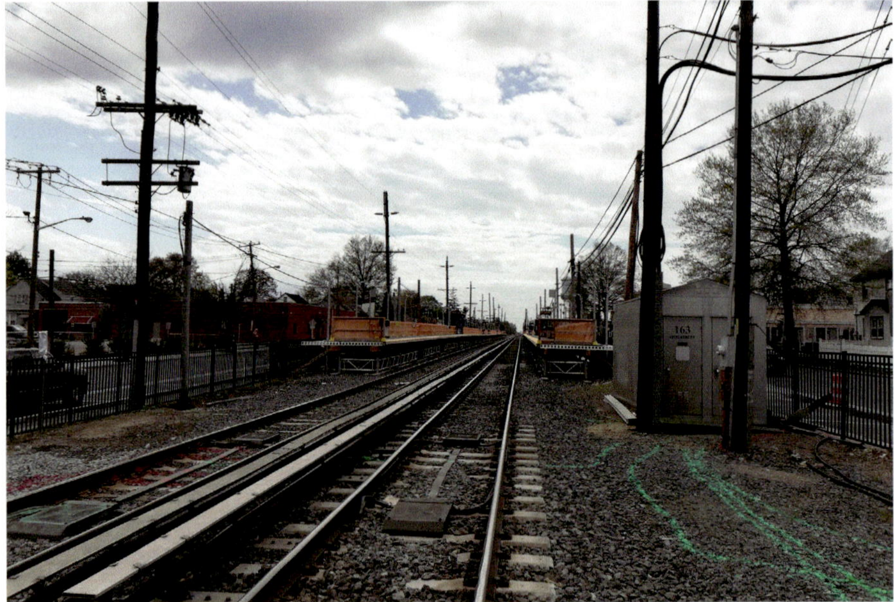

The Third Track program was a massive undertaking that saw an additional track added to the LIRR main line between New Hyde Park and Hicksville to ease congestion and allow for future growth. This photo shows work at the New Hyde Park station in May 2020.

The Santos Mess (2022)

In 2020, an unknown Republican candidate named George Santos ran against incumbent Tom Suozzi for a seat in New York's 3rd Congressional District (parts of eastern Queens and Nassau County). Suozzi won easily, but when he stepped down in 2022 to make an unsuccessful bid for governor, his seat was open and vulnerable, and Santos ran again, facing and defeating Democrat Robert Zimmerman by a margin of 8 percent in the November 2022 election. Questions soon emerged about Santos' background, which seemed to incorporate several lies and exaggerations about his education, experience, and family history as well as his misuse of campaign funds. A groundswell of support for his ouster from Congress grew, and on December 1, 2023, the House voted 311–114 to expel him. A special election was soon announced, to take place on February 13, 2024 (to fill the seat until January 2025). Former Congressman Tom Suozzi announced his intention to run and his candidacy was approved and endorsed by the State Democratic Party. His opponent was Mazi Pilip, an Israeli immigrant of Ethiopian heritage, Nassau County legislator, and relative newcomer to politics. The very short, two-month-long campaign was intensely run, with both sides playing to local fears and hopes in the district. Polls showed a neck-in-neck race, but in the end, Suozzi won handily, 54 percent to 46 percent, thanks to a centrist approach and support in certain very Democratic communities that approached and surpassed 90 percent. His win made national headlines, at the time showing the potential for Democrats across the country to retake Republican seats. Following the election, New York's Congressional District maps were redrawn again, and District 3 was modified slightly to include more Democratic-leaning areas in Huntington. Suozzi won a full term in November 2024, though at a tighter margin of 51.6 percent to 48.4 percent. In 2025, Santos was sentenced to seven years in prison.

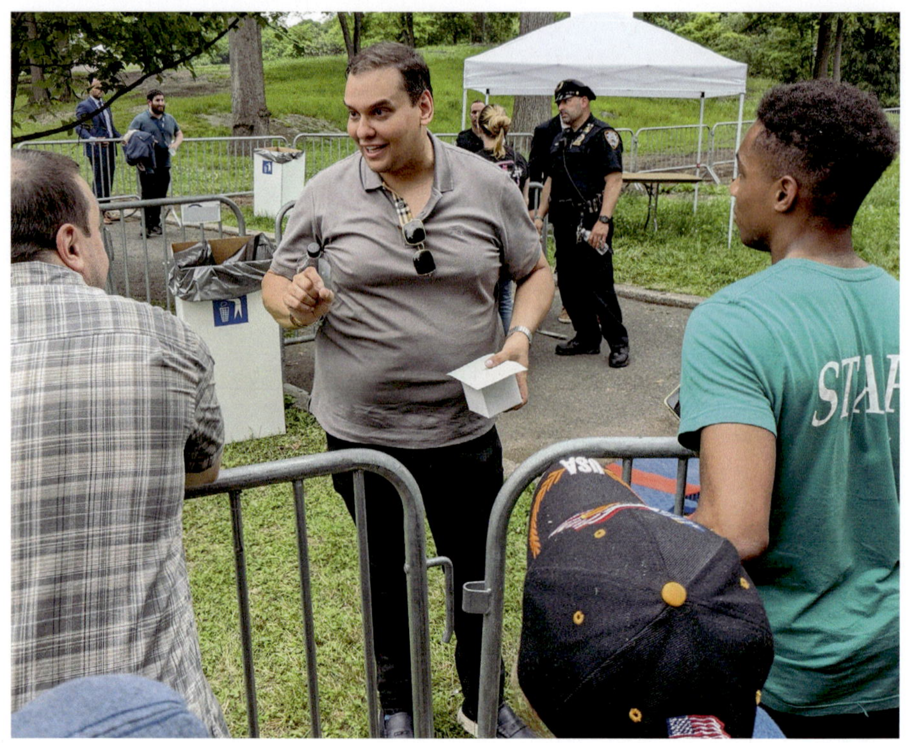

Congressman George Santos (seen here at a Trump rally in the Bronx, May 2024) was ousted from his seat in Long Island's 3rd Congressional District in December 2023 after revelations about his past.

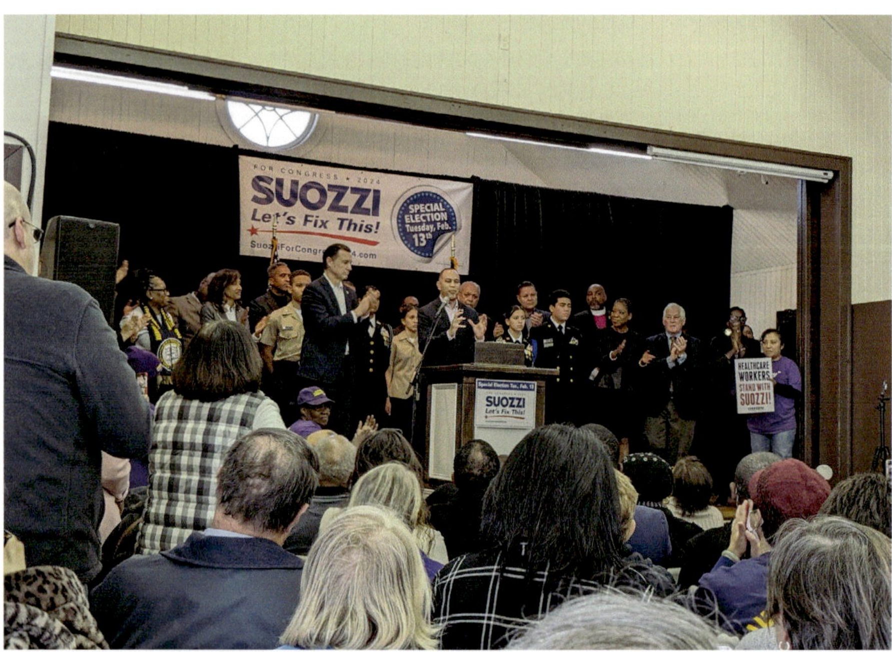

House Minority Leader Hakim Jeffries speaks at a rally for Tom Suozzi in Westbury, February 4, 2024, less than ten days from the special election to fill the vacancy left when George Santos was kicked out of his seat.

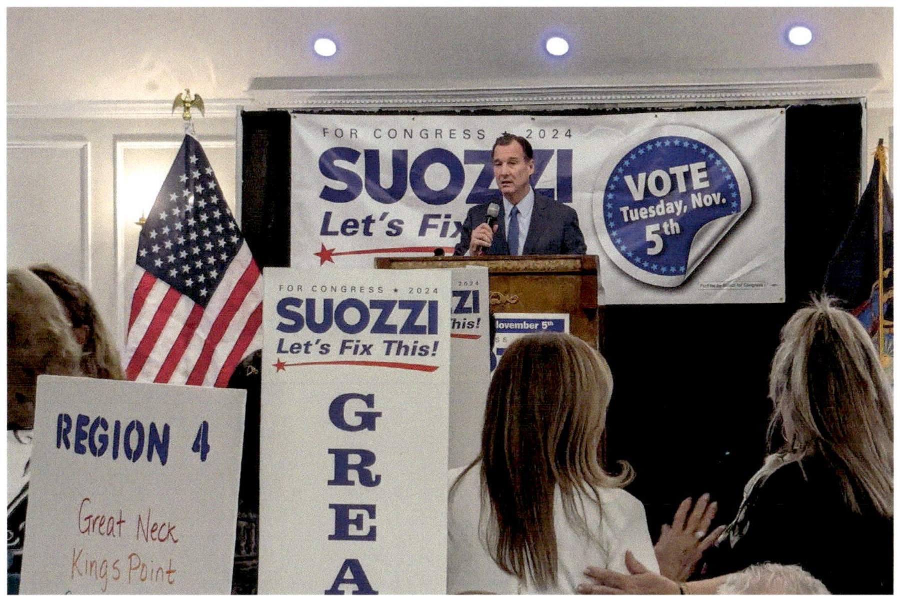

The February 2024 special election allowed Tom Suozzi to serve out the rest of Santos' term; but he had to run again in November 2024 to win a full two-year term. This photo shows Suozzi speaking at an organizing event at the Milleridge Inn in Jericho, September 3, 2024.

Renovated Penn Station (2023)

Though the newly created Moynihan Train Hall is by most accounts a great and inspiring space, there was never any chance that it would completely replace the old Penn Station, as it only allows access to the very western end of train platforms, closest to Eighth Avenue. For Long Island commuters needing to depart their trains closer to Seventh Avenue, the old Penn Station was the way they would continue to experience the Long Island Rail Road. Soon after the new train hall was completed, a major rehabilitation of the old section of Penn Station was begun. The possibilities were limited by the amount of space that was available; no soaring views or grand architectural inspirations were feasible. Still, the plans that were unveiled in November 2021 by Governor Kathy Hochul showed a somewhat ambitious transformation. Once construction began, all retail within Penn Station was shut so both commuter and tenant spaces could be rejuvenated. By late 2023, the first portions of the improved station reopened, featuring a wider main passageway, much higher ceilings, new lighting and signage, and a gradually opening slate of new restaurants and shops. By the summer of 2024, establishments such as Cane's Chicken, Dos Toros, Pret a Manger, Chick-fil-A, Insomnia Cookies, and Starbucks had all opened, with more to come. Improvements also featured a new domed entrance on Seventh Avenue upon which is imprinted a map of New York City.

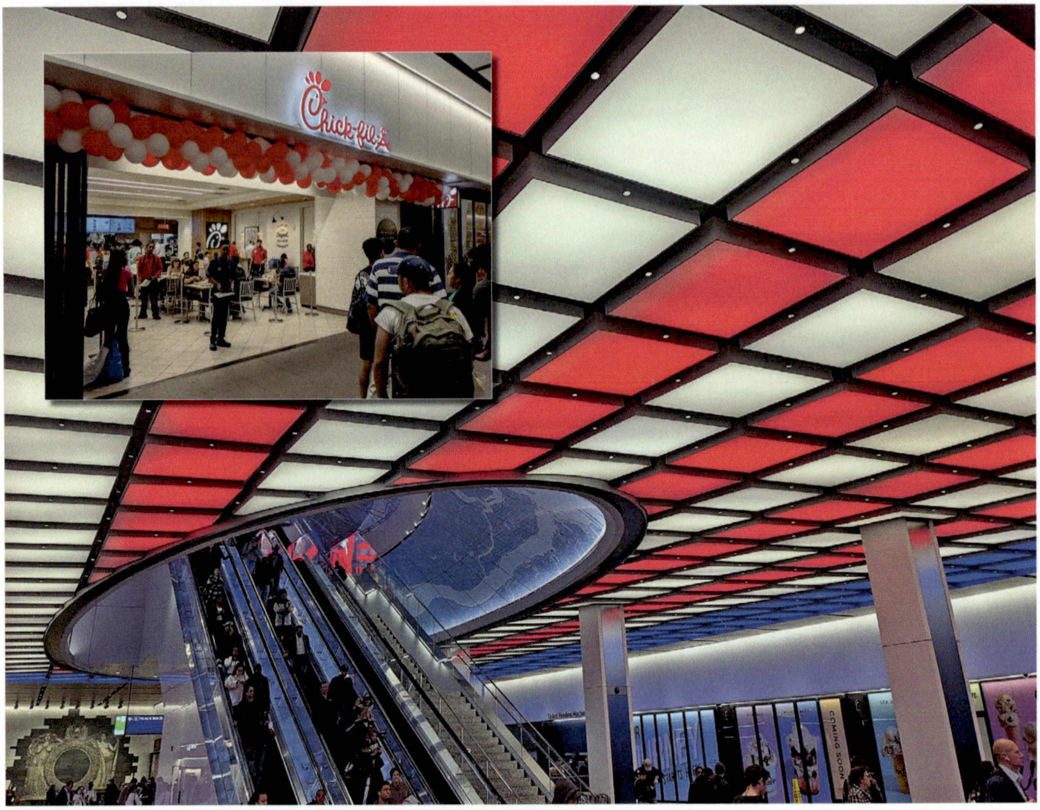

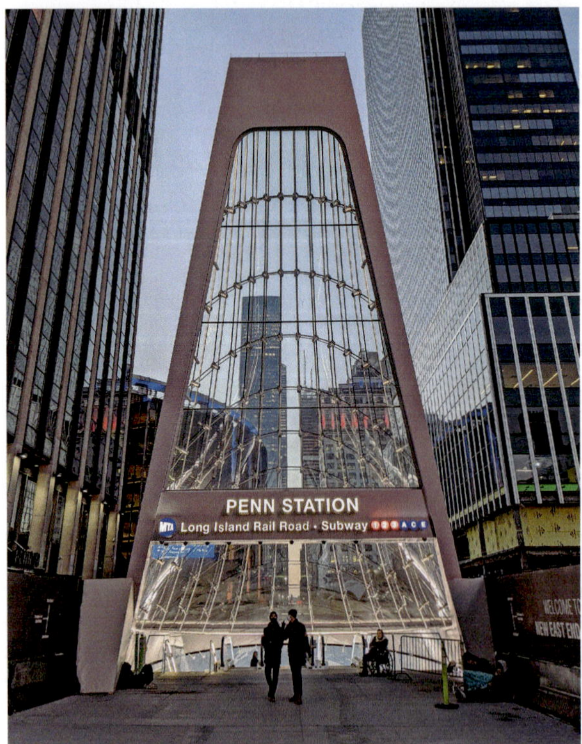

Above: The renovated Penn Station is a friendlier place with higher ceilings and more dining options. The ceiling was lit red, white, and blue on Veterans' Day 2024. Inset: New dining options offer commuters many choices. This photo shows the newly opened Chick-fil-A in July 2024.

Left: One of the first improvements to be made was this new LIRR entrance on Seventh Avenue between 33rd and 34th Streets.

East Side Access/Grand Central Madison (2023)

No matter their ultimate destination, for more than 100 years, Long Island commuters and visitors have always had to end up at 34th Street and Seventh or Eighth Avenues. Anyone wishing to get to the East Side had to take a bus or the 1/9 subway to Times Square and transfer to the Shuttle—until 2023, when the long-awaited Grand Central Madison (aka East Side Access) project was completed. Planning began in 1998 and construction started in 2001, with tunnel construction starting in 2007. The new station opened to full service in February 2023. About 45 percent of LIRR commuters were projected to divert to the new station instead of Penn, saving many of them up to forty minutes from their commute. The new 350,000-square foot Grand Central Madison Terminal is adjacent to and underneath the old Grand Central Terminal and extends from 43rd to 48th Streets, with exits at several points allowing easy access to a wide range of east side locations. In December 2024, Grand Central Madison was awarded UNESCO's 2024 Prix Versailles Interior Award for the World's Most Beautiful Passenger Station category. As of early 2025, the many available retail spaces in the new station had not yet been filled.

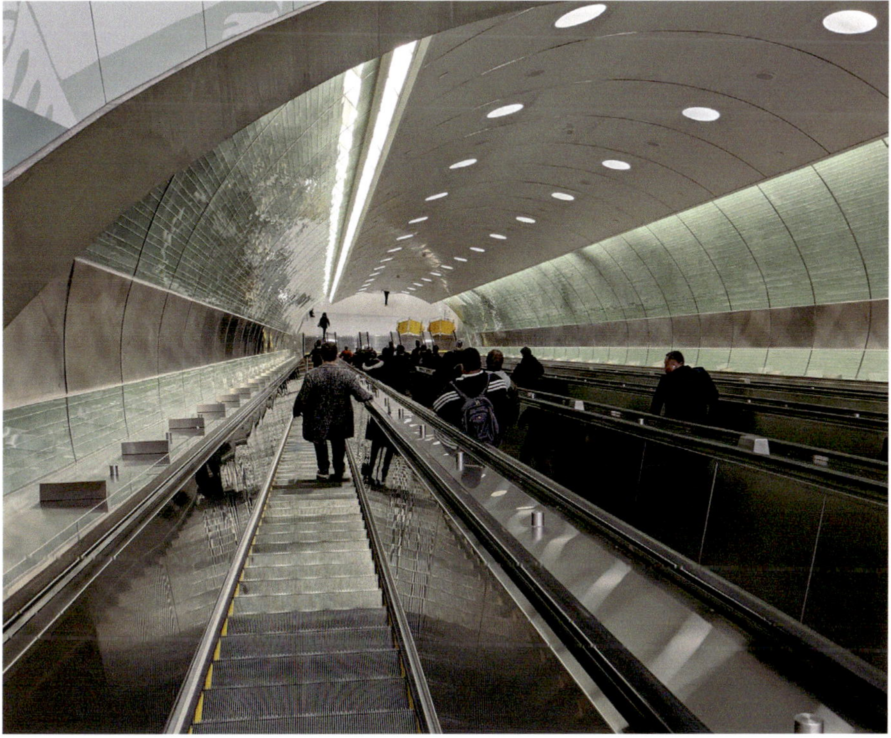

The escalators at Grand Central Madison are 182 feet long and 90 feet tall, the longest and steepest in the city's transit system.

The Cricket World Cup (2024)

In November 2023, Nassau County Executive Bruce Blakeman signed an agreement with the International Cricket Council to build a new (but temporary) 34,000-seat cricket stadium with 75-foot-high grandstands in Nassau County's Eisenhower Park, in a field adjacent to the mini golf courses and the Aquatic Center. The 66-foot-long, 10-foot-wide "pitch" was assembled in Australia and sent to Florida from whence it was shipped to New York. The stadium hosted eight matches for the 2024 International Cricket Committee's T20 World Cup between June 1 and June 12, including the highly touted India *v.* Pakistan contest on June 9. The stadium was built in just 106 days. During this time, the park was closed from 6 a.m. to 6 p.m. and nearby roads were also closed off. Just days before the events were to begin, a threat against the event was received from a pro-ISIS group. Nothing materialized, and the only incident was a fan running onto the field to embrace one of the Indian players before he was subdued by police. Matches included Canada *v.* Ireland, Pakistan *v.* Canada, South Africa *v.* Bangladesh, and the big one, India *v.* Pakistan. After a couple of matches had been played, there were complaints about the pitch being uneven, such that it favored the bowlers. Games were uncharacteristically low scoring. The outfield was also criticized as being uneven. The stadium was dismantled after the event, but the cricket field was to remain. Other World Cup matches took place in Florida and Texas.

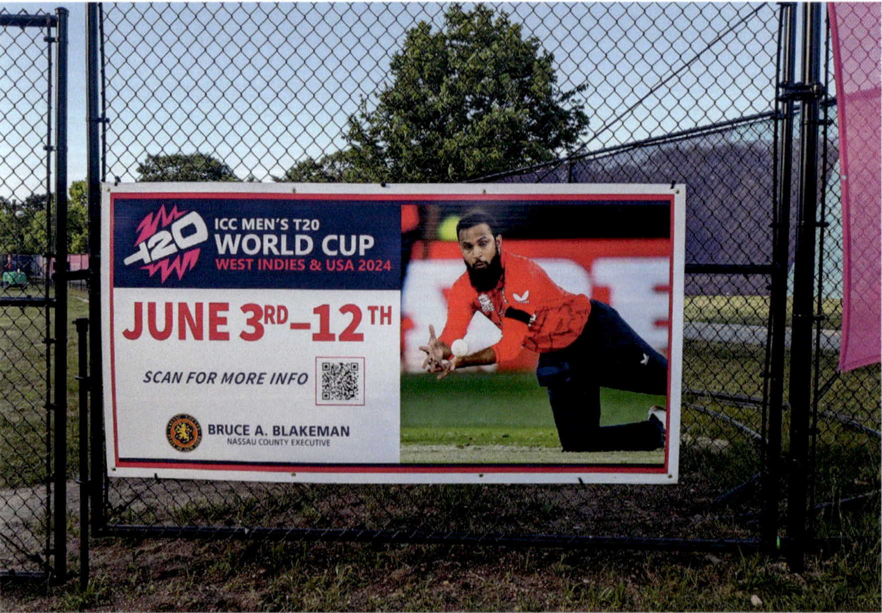

Building the stadium and field for the Cricket World Cup in June 2024 was a fast-track project that was accomplished on time.

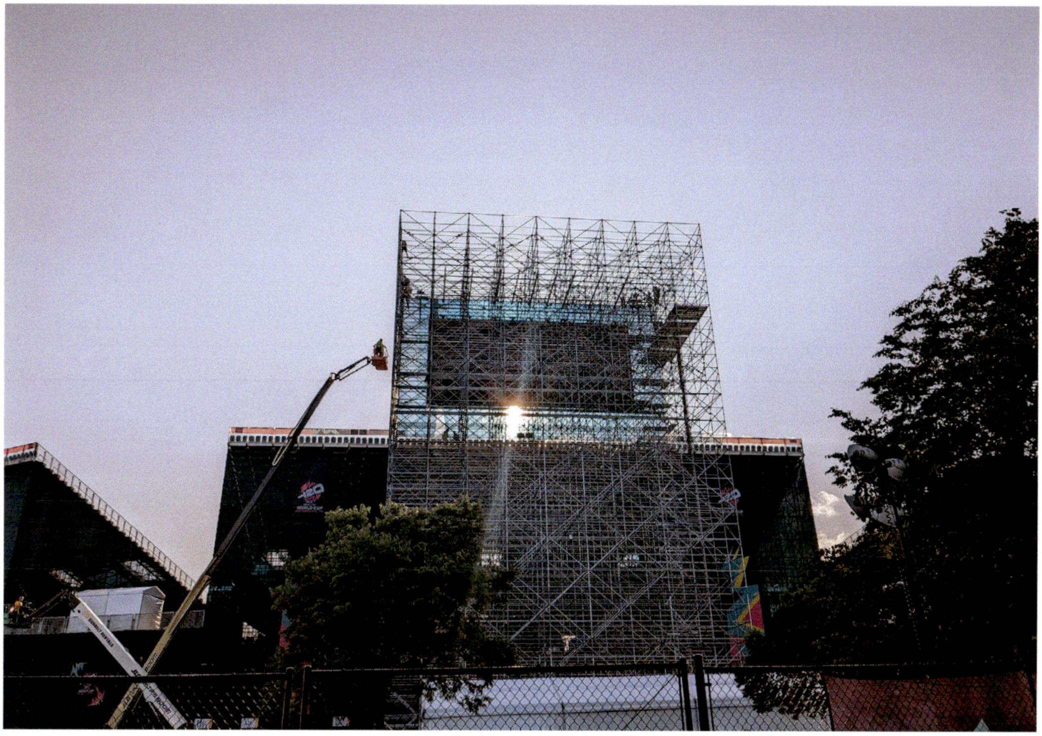

Finishing touches being put on the stadium on May 30, 2024.

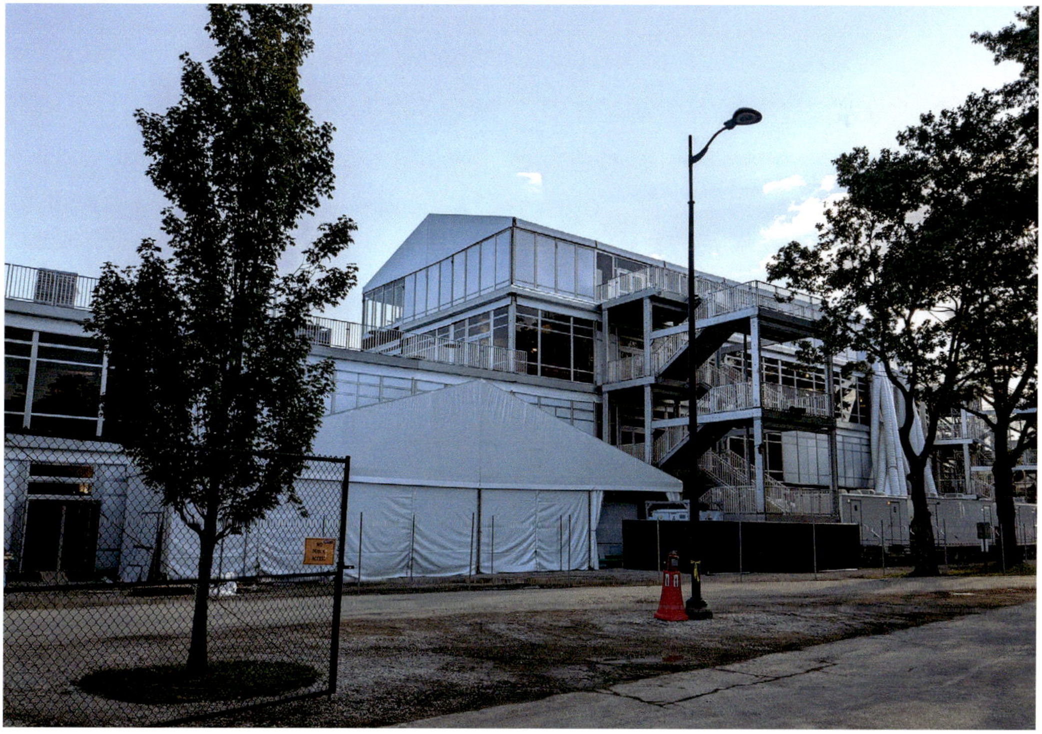

The stadium and its associated structures (see here on May 30, 2024) were dismantled after the event was over.

Long Island Gets a Book Fair (2024)

After Congressman Steve Israel (D) retired from politics by not running for reelection in 2016, he started a bookstore called Theodore's Books in Oyster Bay (in honor of Oyster Bay resident Theodore Roosevelt) in a vacant storefront on Audrey Avenue. An author himself, Israel went on tour around the country and noted how many locations had book fairs—but Long Island had never held one of its own. New York City's Javits Center had hosted the massive Book Expo America for many years until 2020, when the pandemic ended it for good. Israel decided to create a book fair for Long Island and set about inviting a wide range of authors to participate. Held from June 28–30, 2024, on the campus of Long Island University in Brookville and at various locations in downtown Oyster Bay, the fair featured numerous lectures, book signings, and other book-related events by dozens of Long Island authors (including yours truly) with a keynote address by bestselling author Erik Larson (a Freeport native), as well as vendor display tables. Also giving talks were bestselling author Alice McDermott and the Librarian of Congress, Carla Hayden. The fair was a success and ran again in May 2025, with keynote address by biographer Ron Chernow and appearances by romance author Tessa Bailey, legal analyst Jeffrey Toobin, 1969 Met Art Shamsky, and actress Lili Taylor.

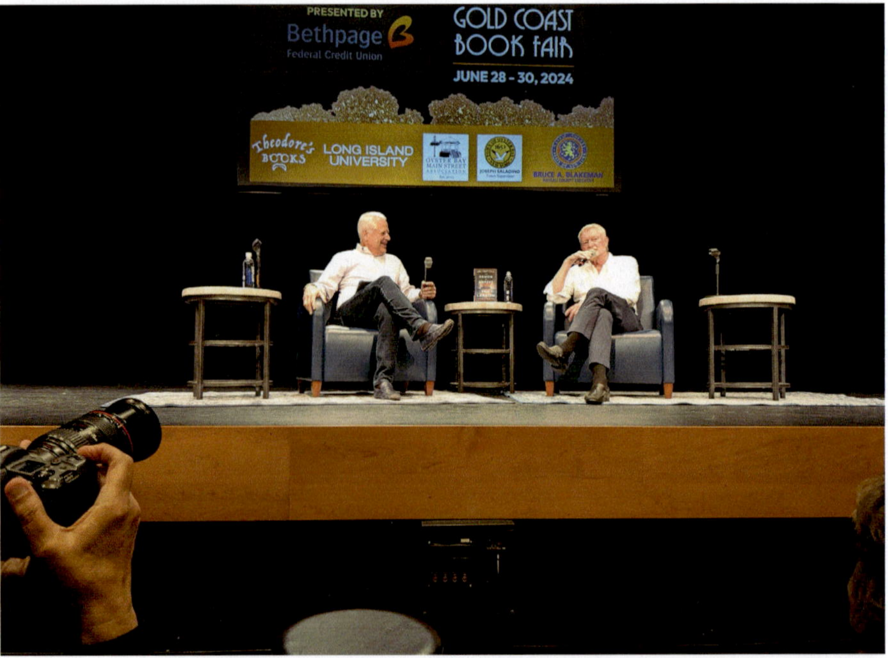

Former Congressman Steve Israel hosts a discussion with bestselling author Erik Larson at the Gold Coast Book Fair, June 28, 2024.

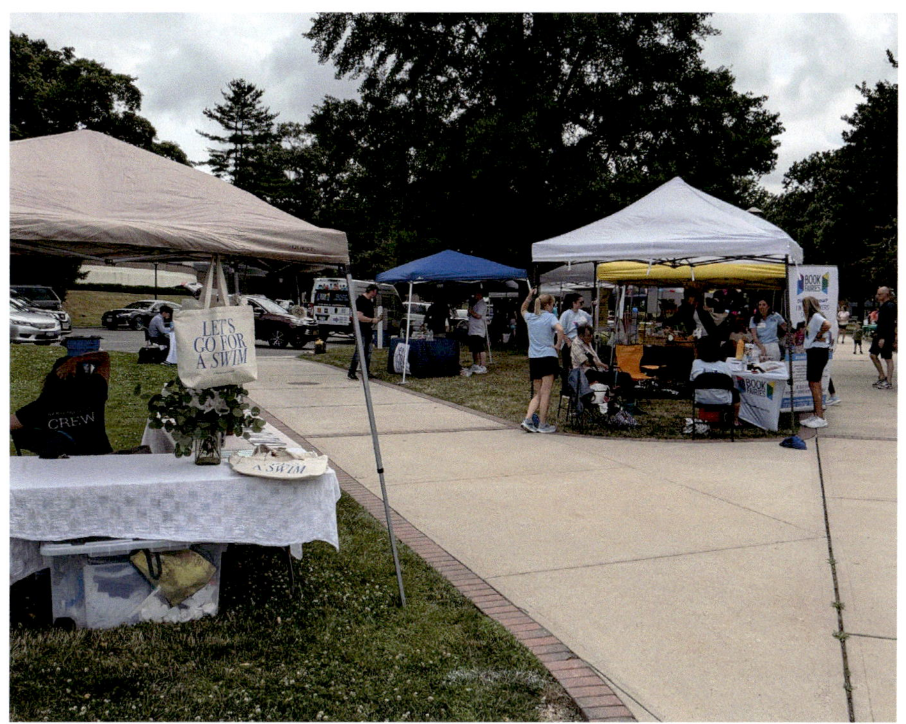

Vendors display their book-related wares at the Gold Coast Book Fair on the campus of Long Island University, June 29, 2024.

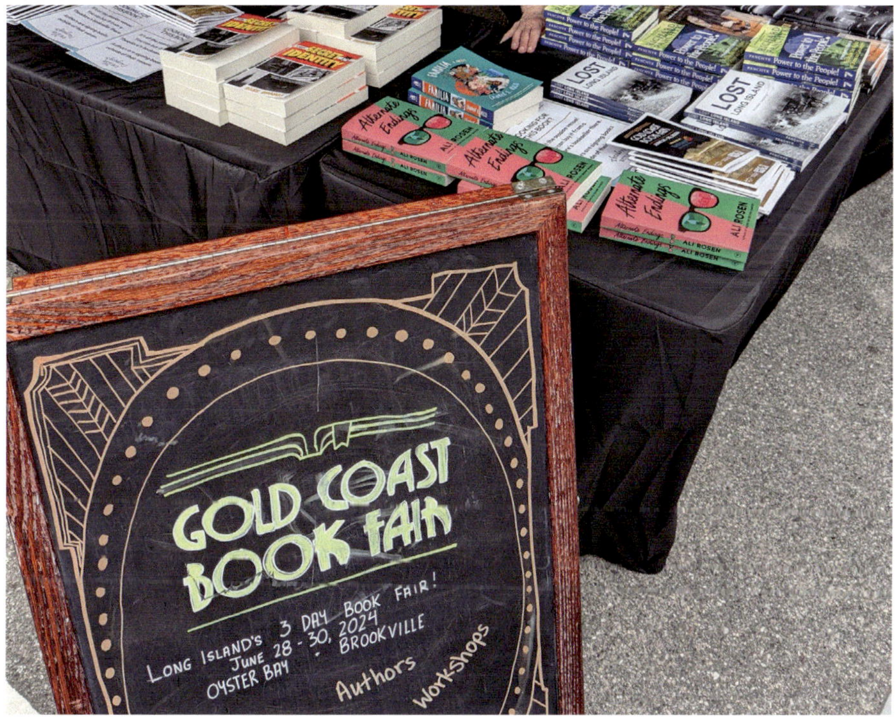

Books for sale as part of the Gold Coast Book Fair in downtown Oyster Bay, June 30, 2024.

Prime Minister Modi Speaks (2024)

On Sunday, September 22, 2024, just a few days after Donald Trump held a rally at Nassau Coliseum, Indian Prime Minister Narendra Modi appeared to speak to the "Indian diaspora"—those of Indian nationality who had left their home country and wound up in the United States. Modi had first been elected in 2014 and was reelected a second time in 2024. About 24,000 people attended the event. The capacity inside the venue itself was about 13,000 instead of the full 16,000 as no seating was allowed behind the stage to protect Modi. According to the County Executive, local hotels were full in advance of the event, with people coming from forty-two states to see the prime minister. Traditional dances and music were also part of the event, but there were some protestors outside by groups who felt marginalized under Modi's rule. The prime minister spoke for a little over an hour, to cheers from an adoring Nassau County crowd. The next day, Modi addressed the United Nations in New York City.

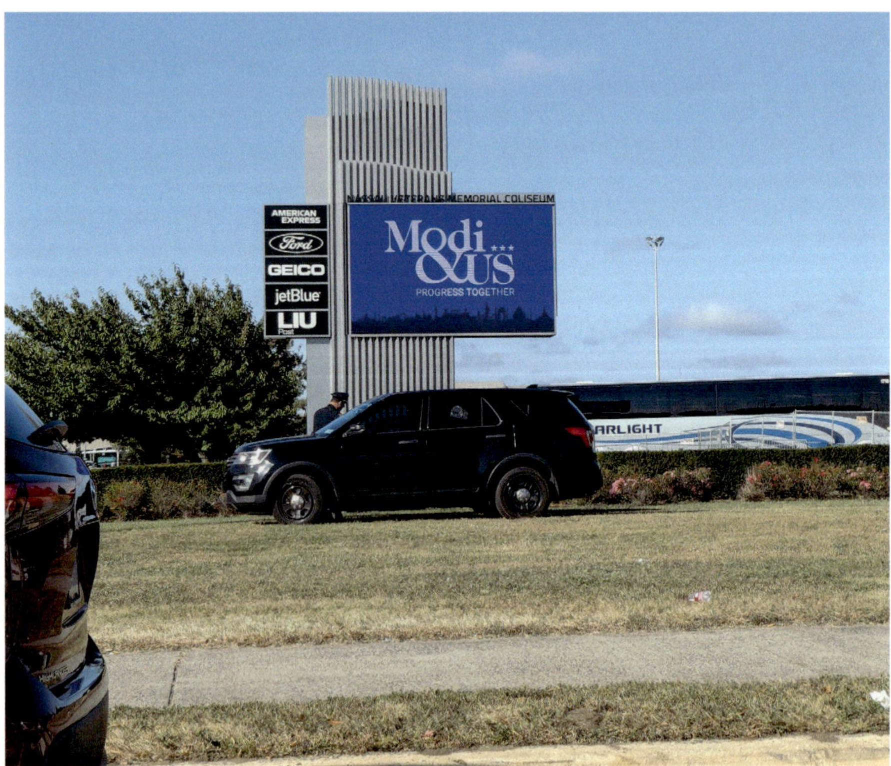

A sign for Indian Prime Minister Modi's visit to the Nassau Coliseum, September 22, 2024.

Northern Lights (2024)

A fast coronal mass ejection (CME) erupted from the sun on the evening of October 8, 2024, arriving at Earth on October 10 and resulting in an extraordinary opportunity for Nassau and Suffolk residents. Late on the chilly evening of October 10, Long Island was treated to quite a visual show. The CME from the sun caused severe geomagnetic disturbances upon arrival, which translated to an intensely bright occurrence of the Northern Lights (aka Aurora Borealis). This ethereal glow was visible at a much lower latitude than the usual northern reaches of Canada. The key for proper viewing on Long Island was finding a north-facing spot with minimal light pollution and a clear view of the horizon. More isolated places along the north shore waterfront were ideal for viewing the phenomenon, which though visible to the naked eye, was more vibrantly viewed through a camera screen and the resulting photographs. The predominant colors of the hours-long light show, which changed hues and patterns by the minute, were green, magenta, blue, and purple.

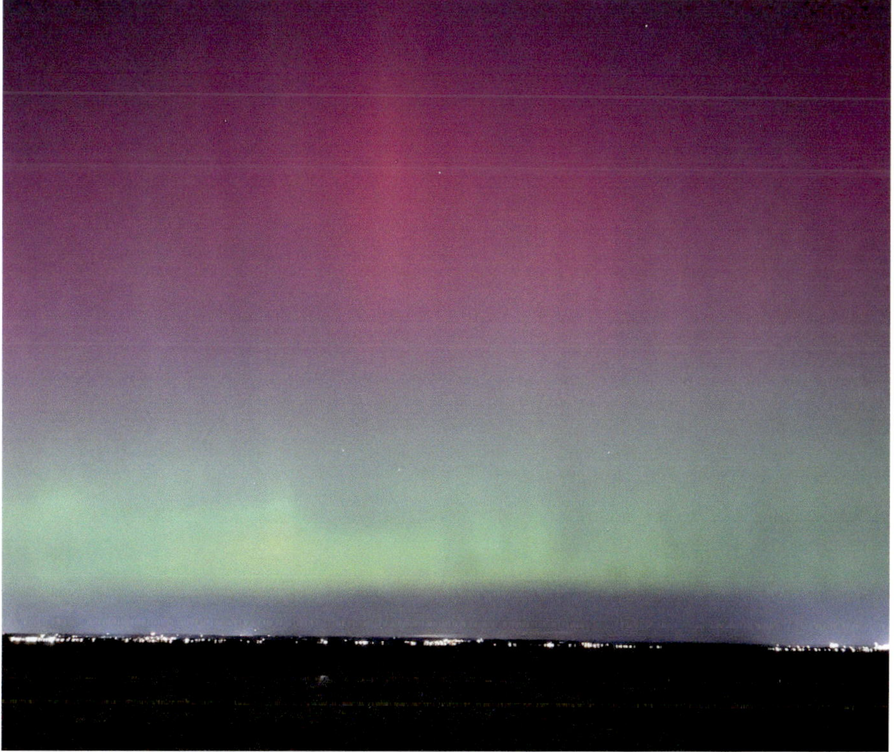

The Northern Lights were widely visible across Long Island on the night of October 11, 2024.

A Farming Comeback (2000s)

During the second half of the twentieth century, farming, once the dominant industry on Long Island, quickly declined as the need for housing increased after World War II and commercial development grew as well. In smaller and more densely packed Nassau County, farming has all but vanished save for a handful of locations including three that sell produce to the public: Youngs Farm (Brookville), Meyer's Farm (Woodbury), and Rottkamp Farm (Glen Head). Suffolk County, though no longer nearly as farm-oriented as it had been, has still been able to foster hundreds of farms due to the sheer size of the county and tourist and resident interest in homegrown produce. Many of the Suffolk farms offer animal attractions geared toward children, including rabbits, llamas, horses, sheep, and geese. Long Island farm produce is also represented in farmer's markets throughout the area, including some in New York City. Though between 2012 and 2017, the number of farms (7 percent) and acreage of farms (17 percent) in Suffolk County both decreased, between 2017 and 2022, there was a 13 percent increase in farmland in Suffolk County and a 61 percent increase in market value of goods sold, with a total of 578 farms on 33,821 acres of land. Long Island farms had about $373 million in agricultural sales in 2022, an increase of 64 percent from 2017. Small farms of 1–9 acres in size make up the highest percentage of Long Island farms.

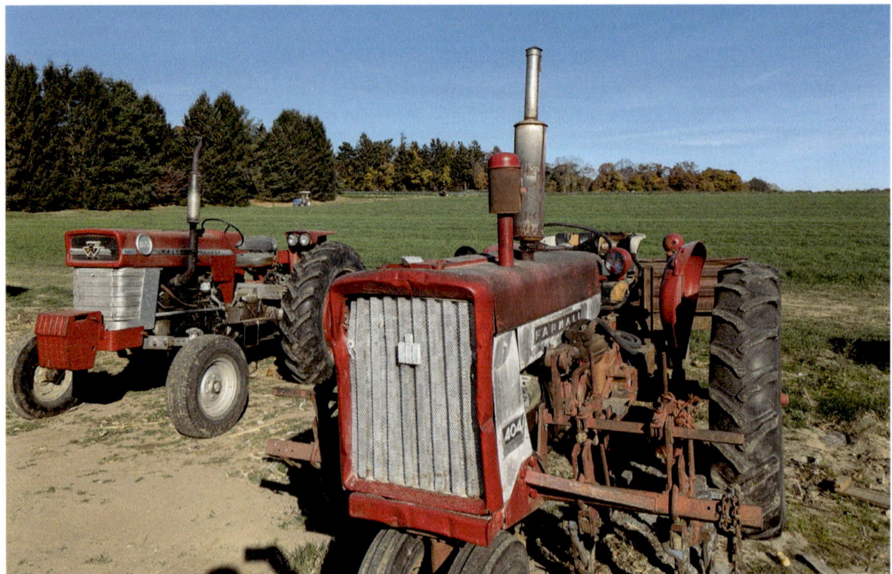

Tractors parked at Rottkamp Farm in Glen Head. The farm is one of only a handful in Nassau County still in operation and offering produce to the public.

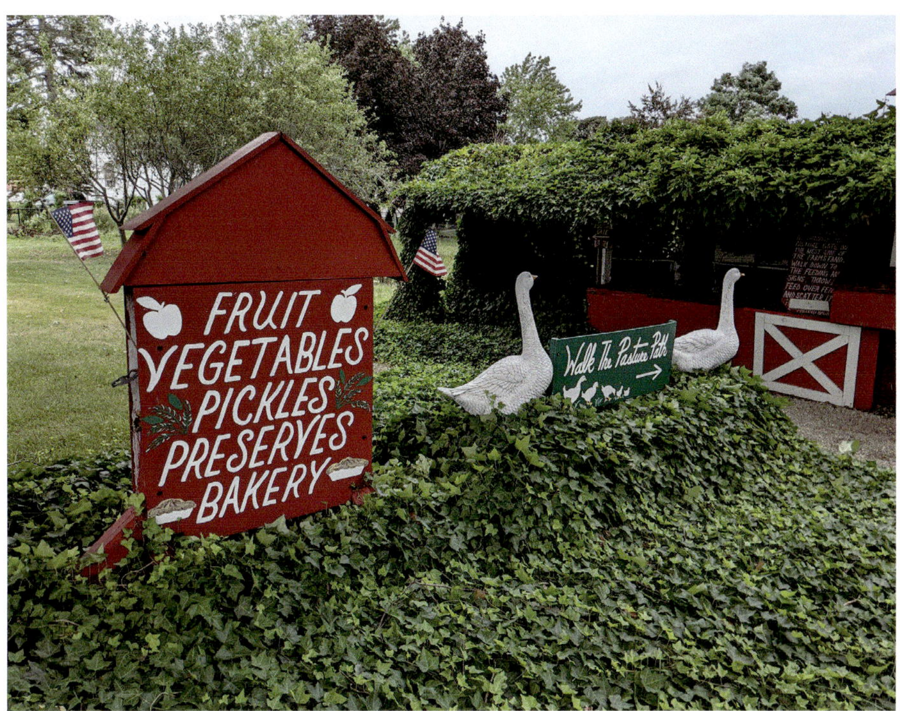

A roadside sign promotes a farmstand in Mattituck. The stand offers fresh produce as well as a chance to view livestock and other animals such as rabbits and geese.

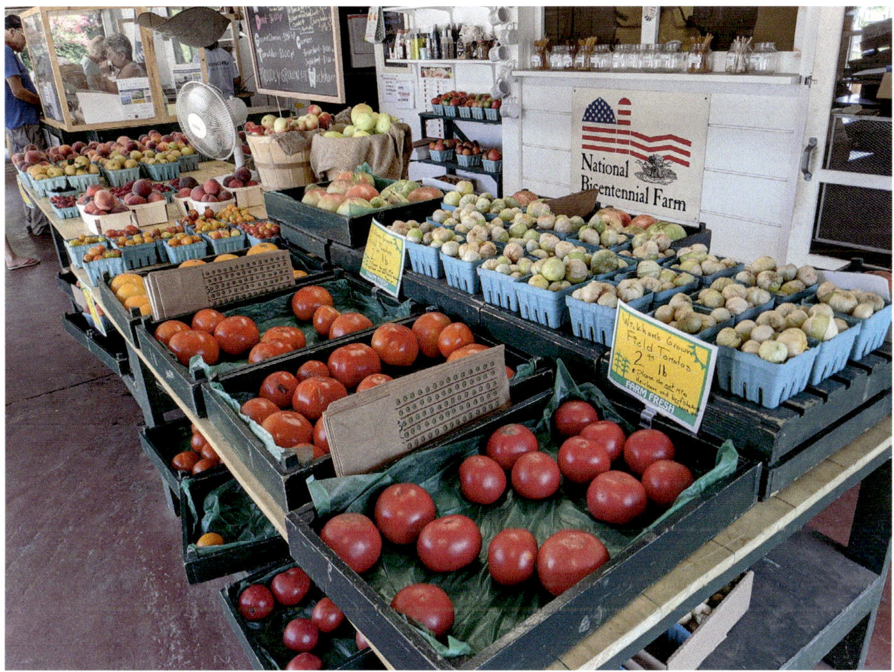

Wickham's in Cutchogue is one of Suffolk county's most popular farm stands, offering fresh produce as well as the chance to pick your own fruit. The Wickham family's presence in the area goes back to the seventeenth century.

The Debate over St. Paul's (2000s)

Built in 1879, the impressive 500-room St. Paul's school for boys was conceived as a memorial to Garden City's founder, Alexander T. Stewart (1803–1876) by his widow Cornelia Mitchell Clinch Stewart (1802–1886). This Victorian Gothic building served as a college preparatory school for some of the nation's most well-heeled children. The school closed in 1991, and the 150-foot-high building was purchased by the Village of Garden City in 1993; it has sat abandoned and decaying since. Since that time, village officials and residents have been unable to agree on the building's fate. Some wanted it demolished; others wanted it saved. In 2003, the Preservation League of New York State put St. Paul's on its list of "Seven to Save" describing the most important threatened buildings in the state. Over the years, many proposals to reuse the space have been put forth (and gone nowhere), including turning it into a condo complex, an assisted living facility, and a library. In 2018, a new proposal was put forth in front of a crowd of hundreds of village residents, to turn the former

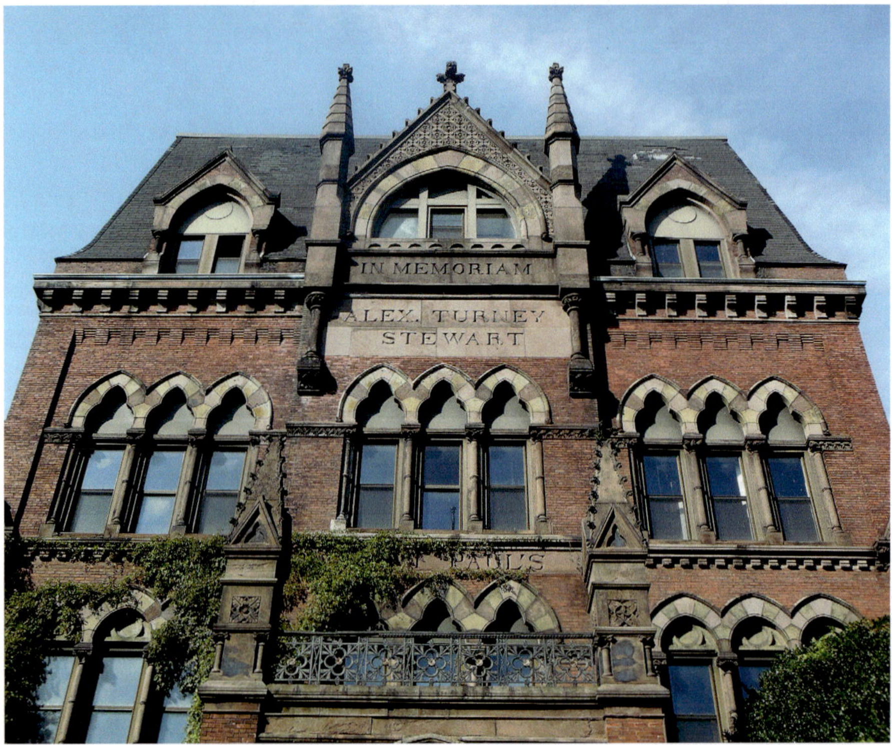

The former St. Paul's School in Garden City (seen in a 2018 photo) is a massive late nineteenth-century architectural masterpiece, but it has been in danger of demolition for years. Locals are hoping to save and repurpose the building.

school into a recreation center with an ice hockey rink as its centerpiece, but that proposal was criticized for its large-scale gutting of the historic building interior. In October 2023, 4,339 Garden City residents participated in a poll to determine support for preservation of the St. Paul's building. The survey results showed 61 percent supported continued efforts by the Board of Trustees to save/preserve the building, and 39 percent supported demolition of the building. As of 2024, the motto of the St. Paul's Advisory Committee was "It's Different This Time"—a reference to optimism over the most recent efforts to save the building *versus* past failed attempts at consensus.

The Rise of the North Fork (2000s)

The Hamptons, Sag Harbor, Amagansett, Montauk, and other South Fork locales have long been the most expensive Long Island vacation and residential locales, but the North Fork was for decades the low-key, lower-priced alternative. During the early twenty-first century, the North Fork began to follow the trend and become a more popular, upscale destination as well. Nowhere was this more evident than in Greenport. Through much of the first quarter of the twenty-first century, the vintage 1950s Silver Sands Motel in Greenport, for example, had remained a stalwart of quieter times—with prices that were under $200 a night in most cases. Following this model, however, the motel was losing money, and the owners were forced to sell. The refurbished and completely renovated motel reopened in 2023. During peak season, prices for a room in the new Silver Sands ranged from $450 to $900 that year. Similarly, the Pridwin Hotel on Shelter Island received an extensive renovation and upgrade starting in 2020; it reopened in 2022 with accommodations priced accordingly. If you wanted to stay the nights of July 5 and 6, 2024, at the Pridwin, it would run you $2,800. More and more upscale boutiques and expensive restaurants began to open in place of more old-fashioned standard fare options. North Fork real estate prices shot up astronomically as well.

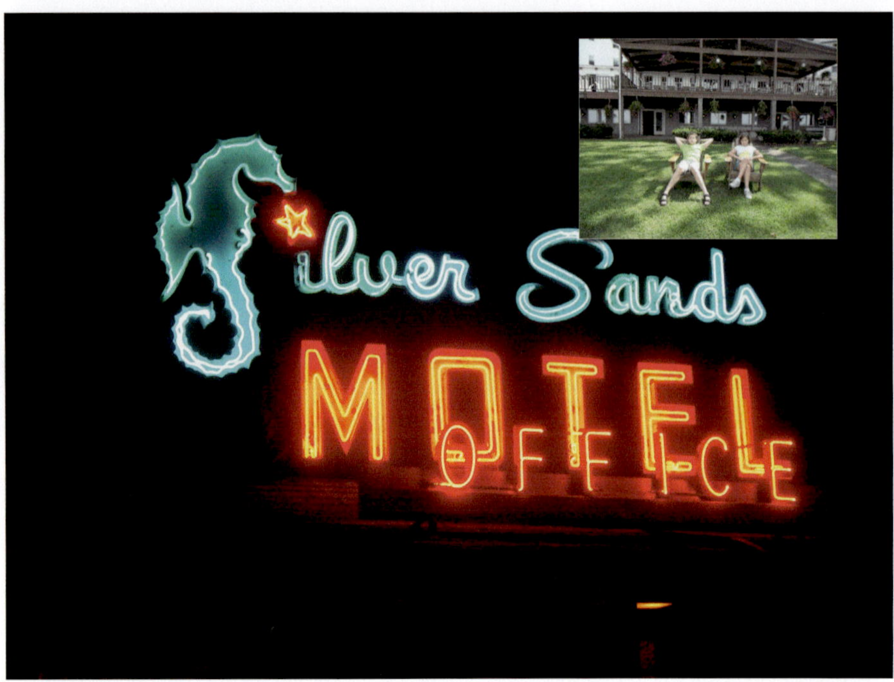

The retro neon sign for the Silver Sands Motel in Greenport, 2010. The motel was sold to new owners and reopened in 2023 with prices reflecting the changing North Fork. Inset: The Pridwin Hotel on Shelter Island, seen in 2011 before its major renovation in 2020. It reopened in 2022.

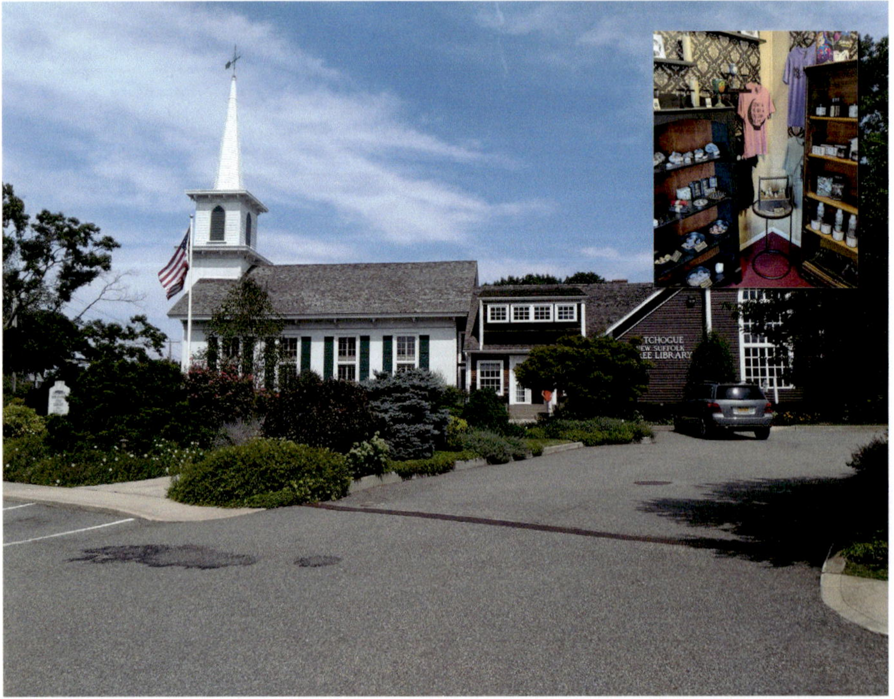

Quaint North Fork downtowns such as Cutchogue attract visitors now more than ever. Inset: Inside a shop in Mattituck. Interesting shops, boutiques, and restaurants line the main streets of North Fork villages.

The Nassau Hub (2000s)

The future of the Nassau Coliseum and surrounding area has been debated for much of the twenty-first century. The area's central location and potentially available land made it ideal for developing into a major mixed-use complex. Nicknamed the "Nassau Hub," this area was viewed as having great potential to serve as a mixed-use center to be served by mass transit, providing housing, shopping, and entertainment. County Executive Thomas Suozzi's vision for the area in 2005 included new office towers, a renovated Nassau Coliseum, and various plazas served by rapid transit buses and a new light rail system. County Executive Ed Mangano's 2011 concept for the Hub included a bioscience innovation center, research and development expo center, office space above retail stores, and residential housing. None of the various development plans and concepts for the Hub gained enough traction (or legislative/ environmental approvals) to be implemented, but some positives have included the founding of the Friends of the Hempstead Plains (2001) and the renovation of the Long Island Marriott (2009). A complicating factor has been the decline of the Coliseum as a concert venue and the relocation of the Islanders hockey team

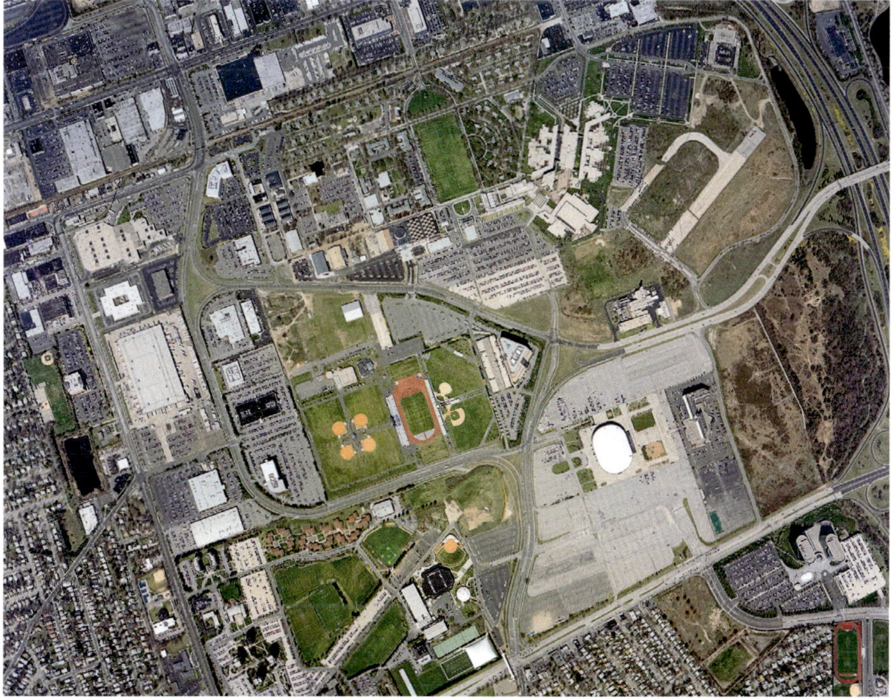

The Nassau Hub area seen in a 2002 aerial view. The white-domed building is the Nassau Coliseum.

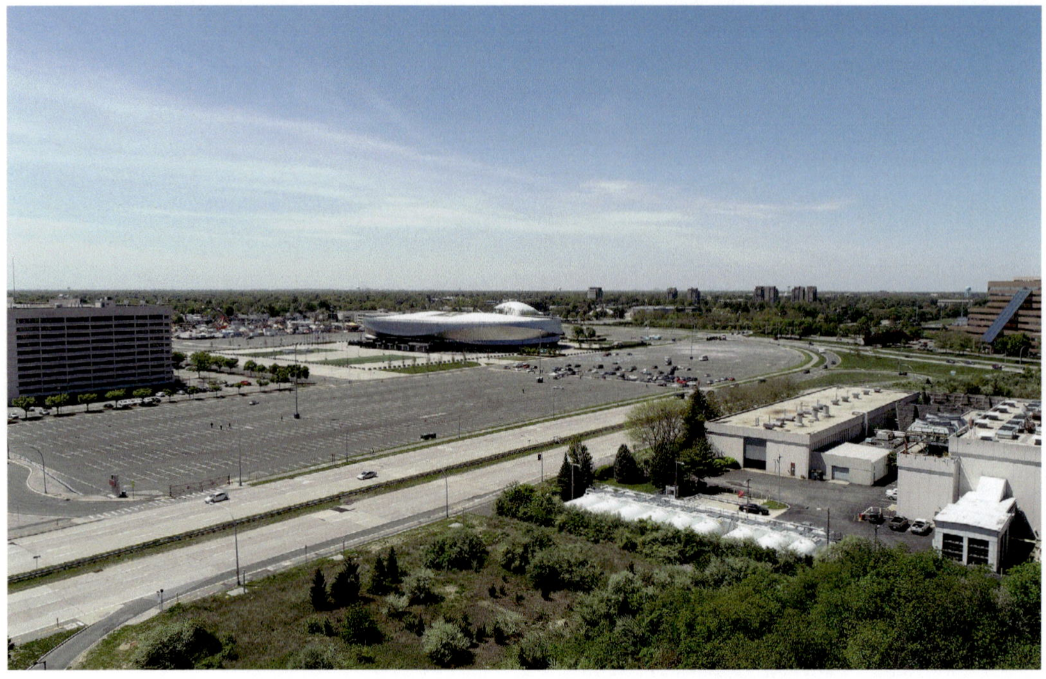

The Nassau Coliseum and neighboring Marriott Hotel. The Coliseum property has been at the center of a long list of proposed development schemes, the latest as of 2025 being the failed attempt at a Sands Casino.

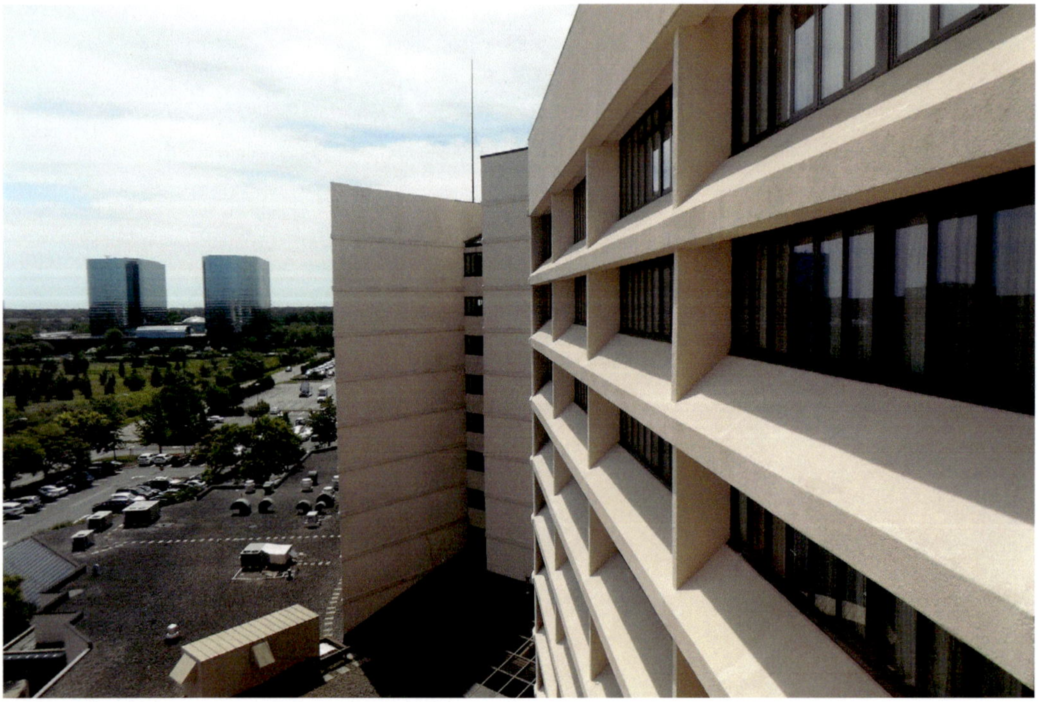

The Marriott Hotel in Uniondale, seen in 2016, is the largest hotel in the area. It used to serve as a perfect overnight respite for visitors to the neighboring Coliseum, which since the opening of the UBS Arena in Elmont has held fewer major events.

with the opening of the USB Arena in Elmont. By 2024, the latest plans for the Hub involved the conversion of the Coliseum and surrounding area into a casino complex operated by Sands, the Las Vegas-based company. A public hearing on the 28,000-page Draft Environmental Impact Statement for the $6 billion casino plan was held in December 2024, with both proponents and detractors voicing their hopes and concerns for the project, which could include an expansion of the Meadowbrook Parkway to allow increased capacity for the traffic a casino would bring to the area. In April 2025, Sands decided not to pursue the project any further.

Vision Long Island and the Smart Growth Summit (2000s)

Founded in 1997, the non-profit group Vision Long Island was created by Northport resident Eric Alexander to educate and advocate for smart growth, including walkable downtowns, sustainable design, transit-oriented development, affordable housing, and green infrastructure. The group works with engineers, architects, planners, the counties, villages, cities, towns, utility companies, advocacy groups, and other stakeholders to provide outreach and gain consensus for a range of projects and programs throughout Nassau and Suffolk Counties. Their Smart Growth Summit held every fall at the Crest Hollow Country Club brings together dozens of local leaders from across the island and across the political spectrum to offer updates on initiatives and participate in panels covering topics such as commercial development, clean energy, and safe streets. Their Smart Growth Awards given out every spring honor Long Island projects and people who have served as models of smart growth principles. Past keynote speakers have included former senator Alfonse D'Amato, Senator Chuck Schumer, Governor David Paterson, and NY State Comptroller Thomas DiNapoli.

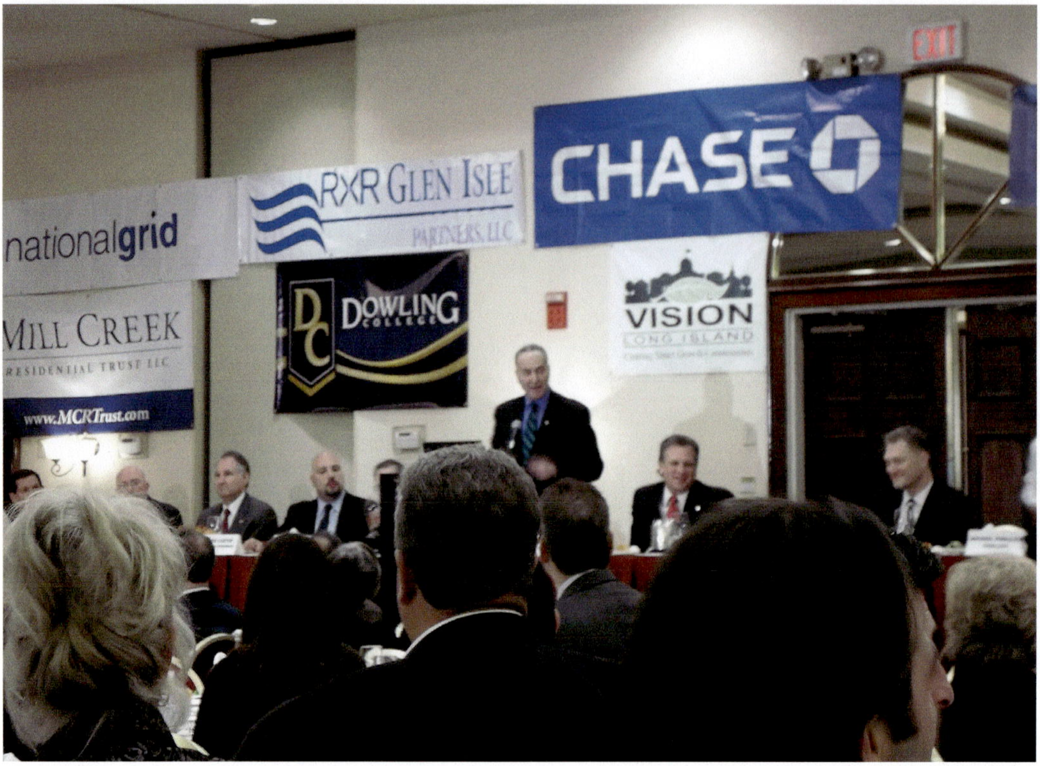

Senator Chuck Schumer (D) speaks at the 2011 Smart Growth Summit at the Crest Hollow Country Club in Syosset.

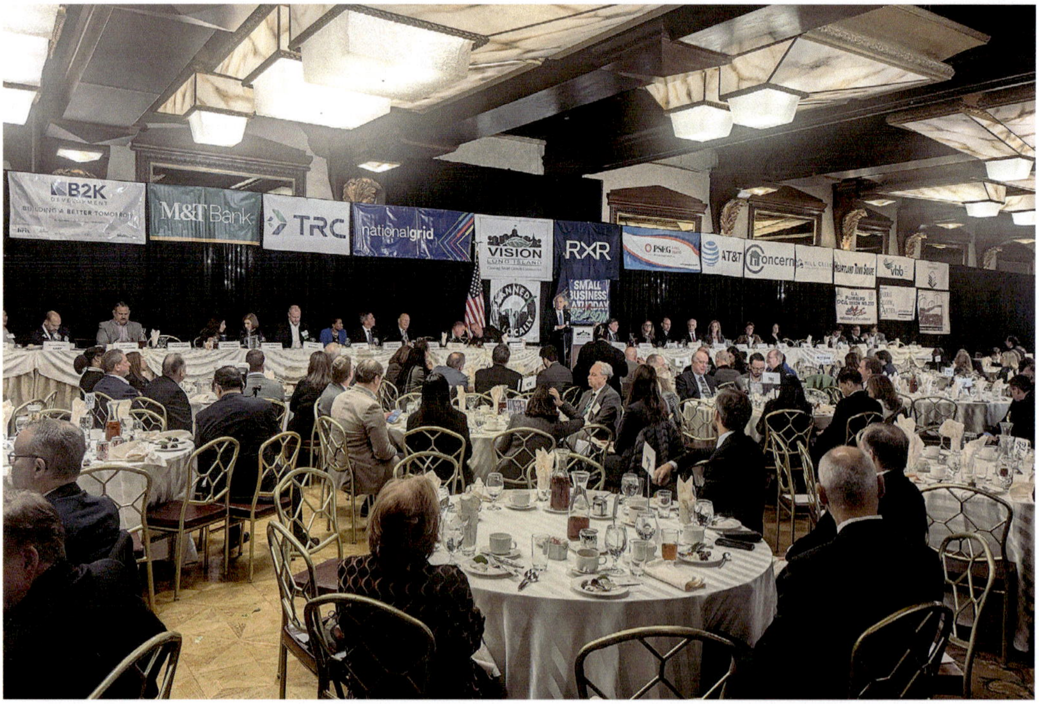

NYS Comptroller Thomas DiNapoli addresses the luncheon crowd at the 2024 Vision Long Island Summit.

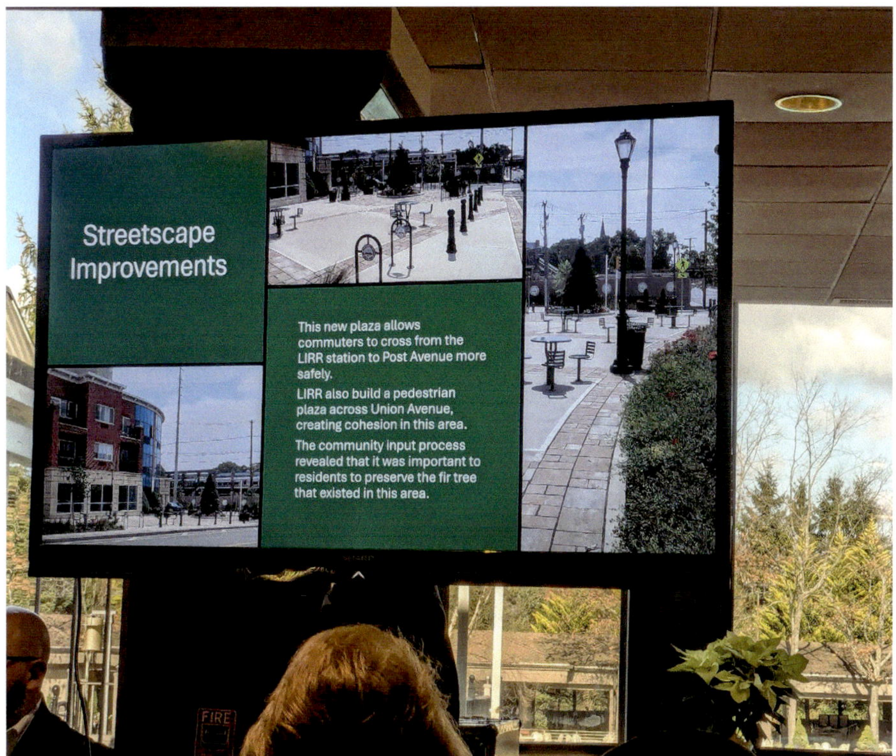

Representatives from villages across the island present as part of a variety of panels during the Smart Growth Summit. Here, a slide on improvements in downtown Westbury is shown at the 2024 Summit.

Resurgence of the Osprey (2000s)

Ospreys are a large bird of prey with a wingspan of 4 to 6 feet. Once relatively common along the northeast coast, the population of the majestic osprey was down to 150 nests between New York City and Boston by 1969. Ospreys were listed as an endangered species in New York in 1976 (due in part to the pesticide DDT, which was killing them and destruction of wetlands that they favored). Thanks to protection (and the banning of DDT in New York in 1971), the birds have made a comeback and are now listed as a Species of Special Concern. Utility company PSEG got involved since these birds of prey often build nests on utility poles; PSEG has worked to relocate more than two dozen nests to avoid danger to the birds and damage to the power lines. There are now about 2,000 active nesting pairs on Long Island. Their nests can be found at dozens of sites across the island. As of 1988, there were just 165 nests from Brooklyn and Queens all the way out to the eastern tip of Long Island. By 2021, there were 460 active nests in the five East End towns alone. Ospreys were downgraded to a Threatened Species in 1983 and a Species of Special Concern in 1999.

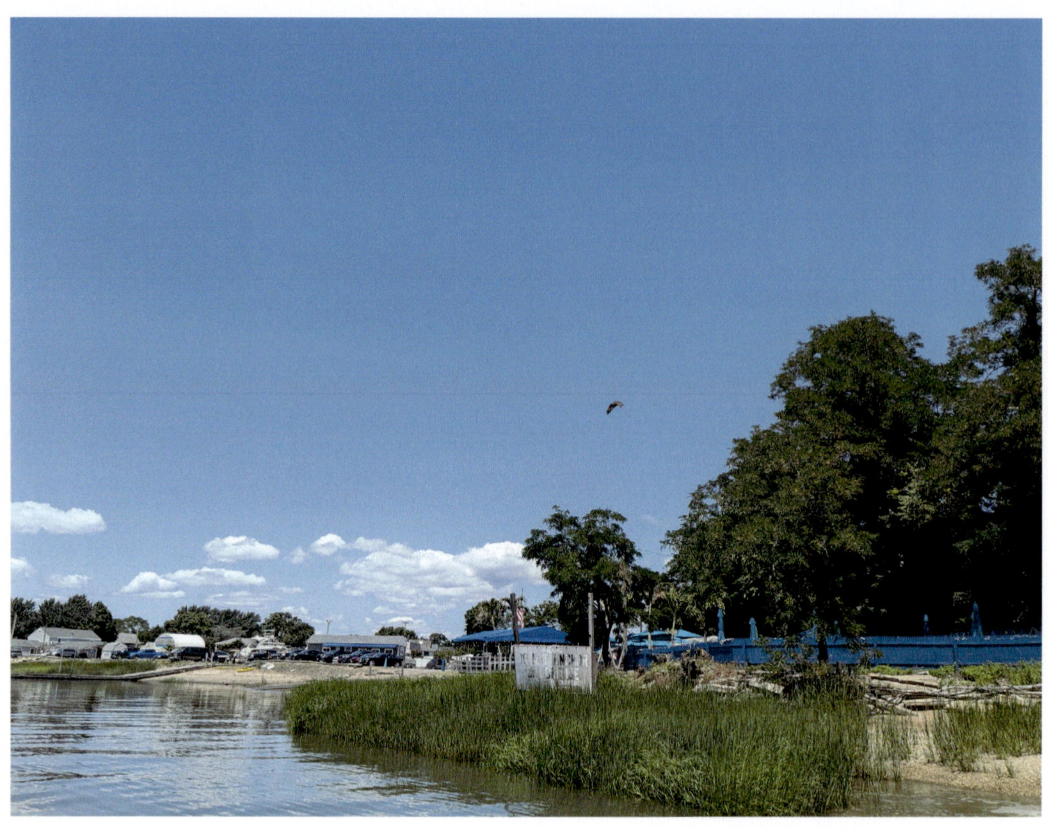

An osprey flies from its nest in Bayville. The osprey's resurgence on Long Island is the result of its protection.

Opposite page: Ospreys prefer high nesting sites such as this pole erected especially for that purpose in Greenport, seen here in 2018. Inset: An osprey in its nest in Greenport in 2014.

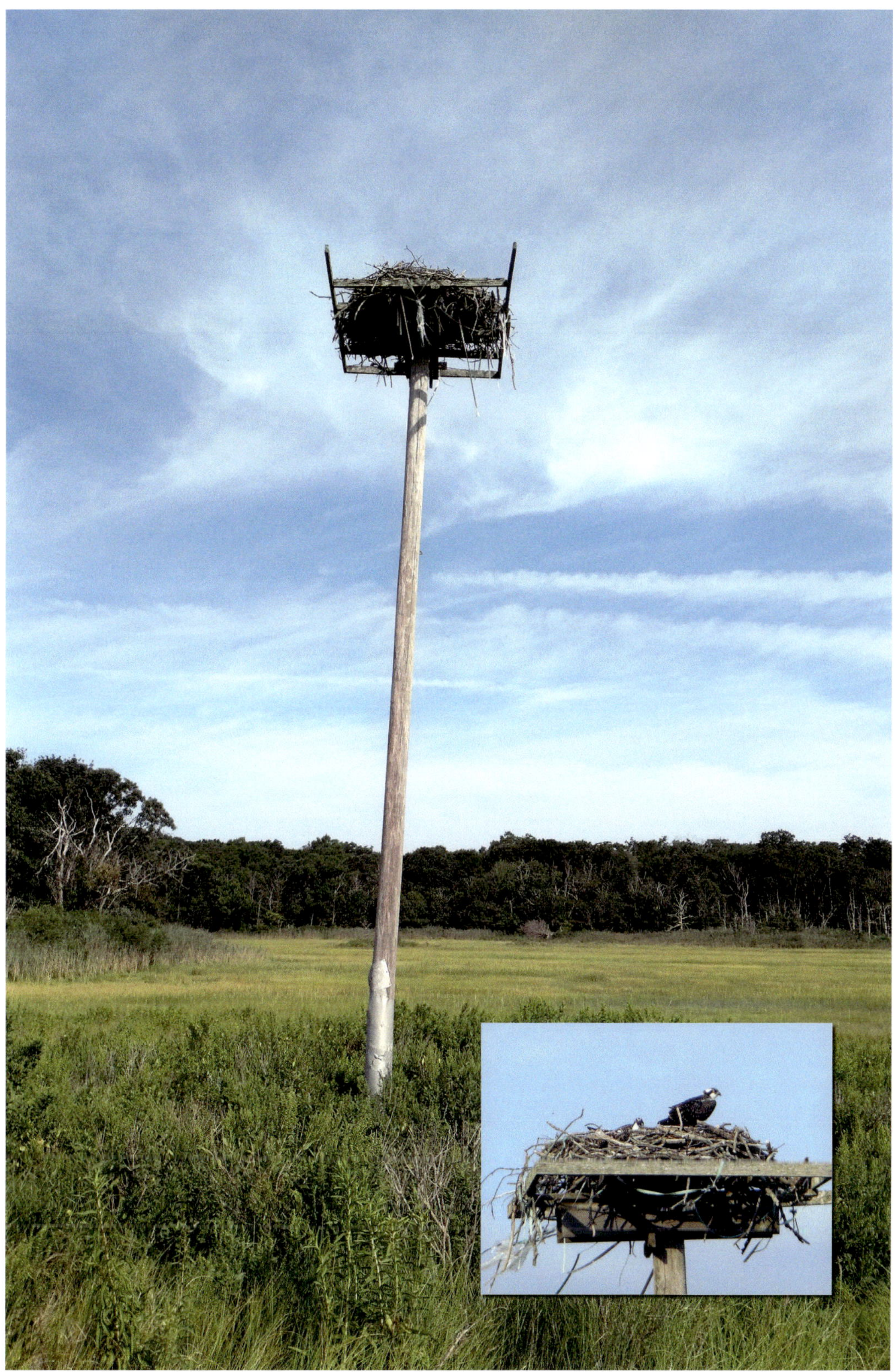